Praise for *The History of Britain Revealed*:

'Witty, provocative, persuasive and original. This book brings a blast of fresh air to British history and liberates the English from a confused creation myth. It made scales fall from my eyes.'   Rupert Sheldrake

'Best re-writing of history since *1066 And All That*.'
Fortean Times

'It is the most outrageous book I have ever read.'
John Michell, *The Oldie*

'Fascinating and deeply learned … I read it twice.'
Norman F. Cantor, Emeritus Professor of Medieval Studies,
Columbia University

'Harper's turns of phrase are delightful, and revisionist readers should enjoy the ride as he twists the orthodox views into knots, from which it looks an increasingly difficult task to extract them.'

The Society for Interdisciplinary Studies Review

'Should come with a health warning – guaranteed to raise the blood pressure of conventional historians.'

History Gateway

THE HISTORY OF BRITAIN REVEALED

THE HISTORY OF

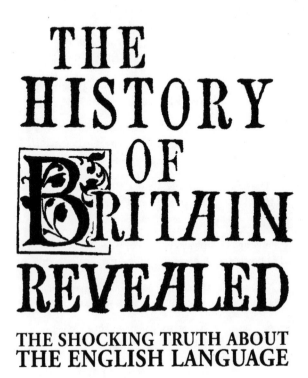

RITAIN REVEALED

THE SHOCKING TRUTH ABOUT
THE ENGLISH LANGUAGE

M.J.HARPER

ICON BOOKS

This expanded edition published in the UK in 2006
by Icon Books Ltd, The Old Dairy, Brook Road,
Thriplow, Cambridge SG8 7RG
email: info@iconbooks.co.uk
www.iconbooks.co.uk

First published as part of the Applied Epistemological
Library by Nathan Carmody, 2002

Sold in the UK, Europe, South Africa and Asia
by Faber & Faber Ltd, 3 Queen Square, London WC1N 3AU
or their agents

Distributed in the UK, Europe, South Africa and Asia
by TBS Ltd, TBS Distribution Centre, Colchester Road
Frating Green, Colchester CO7 7DW

Published in Australia in 2006 by Allen & Unwin Pty Ltd,
PO Box 8500, 83 Alexander Street, Crows Nest, NSW 2065

Distributed in Canada by Penguin Books Canada,
90 Eglinton Avenue East, Suite 700, Toronto, Ontario M4P 2YE

ISBN-10: 1-84046-769-X
ISBN-13: 978-1840467-69-7

Typesetting by Wayzgoose

Printed and bound in the UK by
Creative Print and Design Group

Contents

CHAPTER ONE

An Englishman's Home

According to the canons of English history, the story thus far goes something like this: the Anglo-Saxons, a small and uncultured group of people from a place that can no longer be identified, came over here, replaced the existing population and gave us our language which, what with one thing and another, eventually went on to become the World Language. This gives rise to three possibilities: 1) these 'Anglo-Saxons' are a very remarkable people; 2) history is full of surprises; 3) historians have got it completely wrong. Generally speaking, English people rather favour the first explanation, though they have learned over the years that it's bad form to bang on about it; professional historians are adamant that the second explanation applies, since they are firmly of the belief that there aren't any General Rules of History – it really is a matter of 'one damned thing after another'. This book advances the third possibility. That is because in reality this isn't a book about history at all, but about something called *Applied Epistemology*, a kind of revisionist approach which, stated briefly, believes that everybody gets everything wrong. Or at any rate it sometimes seems that way.

Creation myths are always a little on the strange side because of the mismatch between what is actually known – nobody at the time seems to record these epochal events – and what is urgently *required* to be known: 'Tell us, for God's sake tell us where we came from. And make sure we're special.' Of course, academics are meant to stand fast against the tide of popular passion and point out the truth: 'Sorry, we'd like to help, but it's all lost in the mists of time, you'll just have to put up with not knowing.' However, academics aren't an especially hardy race, and of course they are dependent on the public purse so, not surprisingly, they tend to endorse the public's view. Actually this isn't quite fair. Even an Applied Epistemologist would concede that it's largely down to potty training: historians who write English history tend to be English, so they arrive at the job fully primed in all the myths of English history. When you are born with a certain view of events, and if that version is taught formally to you at school by authority figures, then repeated to you as an undergraduate by even more highly regarded authority figures, and all your colleagues agree that it's more or less self-evidently true, and you'd probably get the sack if you took serious issue with it … you tend pretty much to go along with things. Unless, that is, you're an Applied Epistemologist and were taught that paradigm theories of academic subjects (not to mention religious dogmas, political ideologies, medical axioms, theories of child-rearing and all the other branches of organised knowledge in the real world) tend of their nature to be untrue – though often usefully untrue. Once you are armed with this insight, unravelling the proper History of Britain, or at any rate a less improper History of Britain, is reasonably straightforward. This is largely because the professional historians, archaeologists, palaeo-anthropologists, palaeolinguists, Anglo-Saxonists et al. have spent years and years doing all the necessary spadework on our behalf. Thanks chaps, now clear off, we won't be needing you on this voyage.

Let's take a simple example of how this all operates in practice. Most of us have picked up the story about Pope Gregory seeing Angle 'angels' in the slave market in Rome and thereupon deciding to send (Saint) Augustine to Britain to convert them to Christianity. This is, of course, not history in the sense of being a contemporaneous statement, but it is 'history' in the sense of being 'an early tradition', i.e. a reflection of events as seen by near-contemporaries – Pope Gregory really did send St Augustine off to England to convert the Anglo-Saxons. So it takes its place in the British Creation Myth. But Applied Epistemologists would point out two very odd things about this story, as an episode in the Anglo-Saxon takeover of Britain:

1. Gregory thought the Angles were 'angels' on account of their blond hair which, as a south Scandinavian race, is reasonable enough; but blond Britons are today a small minority.

2. The Angles were pagan and therefore definitely in need of conversion; the population of Britain at the time of Pope Gregory had been Christian for many centuries.

What is really happening here is that two rather different strands are being quietly conjoined: that the native population of Britain was converted from their 'Celtic' form of Christianity to the Roman variety; and that their 'Celtic' language was replaced by Anglo-Saxon. And the two go rather nicely together. Furthermore, the proof is all around us: the British were still Roman Catholics a thousand years later, and today we are all speaking Anglo-Saxon (or English as we prefer to call it.) All very obvious, except that the whole thing rests on an assumption that is never examined: *that English is a modern form of Anglo-Saxon.*

This book belatedly gets round to examining whether this is true or not. Actually that's a pretty narrow, technical question – 'Is English Anglo-Saxon?' – but, as things turn out, a negative answer leads to all kinds of changes in British history; and those changes cannot be contained to Britain, but start infecting some equally unexamined assumptions in European history. Before you know it, vast chunks of history are having to be rewritten along with even vastier chunks of linguistic theory. It's easy! It's fun! It's even quite important if these things matter to you. But that's what we Applied Epistemologists do: we take a subject (any subject except ones in which the scientific method operates effectively), we disassemble it down to its basic paradigms, we examine these paradigms and if we burst out laughing we know we're in business.

So first, the official basic version of British linguistic history, for those who weren't paying attention or who went to schools that believe in 'relevance' and teach Europe 1919–45 every year until even the dullest can get through their GCSE:

End of the Ice Age
British Isles are gradually populated from Europe by people called Cro-Magnons. Hunter-gatherers. Language unknown.

5000 BC

New group moves in from Europe, introduces agriculture. They build considerable monuments, e.g. Skara Brae, Newgrange, Stonehenge. Probably speaking an Indo-European language.

1000 BC

Celtic-speakers move in, probably originally from the Danube delta, but have already occupied a wide swathe of Europe. They are speaking languages ancestral to Welsh, Scots Gaelic, Cornish, Erse.

250 BC

Another Celtic-speaking group, the Belgae, occupy southern and eastern England. Native languages not affected.

50 AD

Romans occupy England, Wales and (for a while) southern Scotland. Natives continue to speak their various Celtic languages.

450 AD

Romans leave. Anglo-Saxons start arriving on the east coast and gradually start pushing the Celtic-speakers westwards. By some undetermined stage, Anglo-Saxon-speakers have replaced Celtic-speakers throughout the whole of England (apart from Cornwall), the eastern half of Wales and the southern half of Scotland.

900 AD

Viking invasions. Anglo-Saxon states replaced by Danish ones (though it's a bit back-and-forth). No change in the local language situation.

1066
Anglo-Saxons replaced by Normans permanently in England, somewhat later and looser in Scotland. Anglo-Saxon gradually develops into English in England and into 'Lallan Scots' (what we know as Rabbie Burns dialect) in lowland Scotland. Cornish, Welsh, Scots Gaelic continue in their areas.

13th, 14th centuries onwards
In both England and Scotland the governors, as well as the governed, have become English/Lallan speakers. Wales conquered by English. Celtic minorities in Cornwall, Wales and Scotland gradually pushed northwards and westwards.

18th century onwards
Cornish disappears entirely. Scots Gaelic holds out in the far highlands and islands, Welsh remains viable in west Wales. All English dialects, including Lallan Scots, become standardised (more or less) around the London/South Midlands variant.

If this Received Version is true, or even if it's a properly constructed academic theory based on the evidence, we would expect a few anomalies to be present where gaps in the evidence have led historians into error (or where history is just plain anomalous); and since pre-history and early history are areas in which there are particularly wide gaps in the evidence, we would expect to find quite a lot of these anomalies. On the other hand, given that the history of Britain is of widespread public interest and Britain has rich academic resources to deploy in the satisfaction of that interest, we would also expect these anomalies to be under constant, intense scrutiny and, one by one, to be resolved.

But if this is *not* a properly constructed academic theory, if it is in fact little more than a creation myth, we will observe quite a different pattern. The evidence will still flow in from the routine day-to-day work of the professional practitioners, so the gaps in the evidence will be progressively narrowed, but – because creation myths always have a more or less permanent hiatus between 'what happened' and 'what *is fondly imagined* happened' – the anomalies will *not* disappear. On the contrary, they will tend to stand out in more and more glaring relief since it will become increasingly difficult to hide them under that all-purpose academic defence to acknowledged anomalies: 'More research is needed.' This is an uncomfortable situation for academics who are paid to resolve anomalies, not make them worse.

The treatment of anomalies is a chief difference between Applied Epistemologists and academic specialists. To the latter, an anomaly is simply *something of interest* within his field of study. He may personally be involved in its resolution; more likely he will merely assume that others are working on it and that resolution will come about sooner or later from general advances in his subject as a whole. But even if it doesn't, even if the problem is never satisfactorily resolved, he is hardly likely to throw out the whole just because some part won't fit. The classic example of this was the perturbation of Mercury's orbit. For hundreds of years it was known that Mercury wasn't behaving exactly according to Newtonian physics. And for centuries it was assumed that 'observational error' was the cause of the anomaly and that it would be cleared up as soon as observational methods were sufficiently advanced. Applied Epistemologists would have pointed out that observational methods *had* advanced for centuries and the anomaly remained, so it couldn't be down to observational methods. No, the Newtonian Universe would have to be thrown out instead. Finally Einstein got round to agreeing with them.

So the specialists have a problem. An unresolved anomaly means there's something seriously wrong with the subject. But there can't be anything seriously wrong with the subject because it has to be taught in an authoritative way to students on a daily basis. Can you recall a teacher or lecturer striding into the room and announcing, 'What I am going to say now is probably a bunch of bollocks but you've got exams to pass and I've got a mortgage to pay, so just listen up'? Thus, whenever creation myths – whenever false academic paradigms in general – are present in any field of study, academics start to suffer from (what other academics have termed) 'cognitive dissonance', the blank refusal to recognise that any problem exists, accompanied by a shrill defensiveness towards anybody who thinks otherwise. Which can often include most of the general public, but they tend to react with their own version of cognitive dissonance, the embracing of theories that are even more extravagantly anomalous, in fact downright crazy. This in turn is of great assistance to the professionals, since anything that has the 'crazy' label attached to it can be resolutely ignored anyway.

With fewer and fewer professional investigators concerning themselves with the anomalies, the whole business becomes increasingly marginal to the subject as a whole. When the anomalies have persisted for a certain length of time, inquiries about their current status will be met with, 'Oh, no, not that old chestnut again', until eventually they fall so far off the academic radar screen that few present practitioners are even aware of their existence. The best that can be hoped for is a backwater in which a handful of elderly scholars battle listlessly with one another while sensible academics, with careers to make, head off for greener pastures where all the other over-fed cows are munching away on the grass growing out of their own manure.

All of which makes for a stable, if palsied, position, since with little professional activity data will always remain *relatively* scarce and thus complaints about anomalies can always be met with 'More research is needed' – which is of course true, and will indefinitely remain so. In the unlikely event that public interest – that is, public dissatisfaction – becomes so strong that outbreaks of truly crazy hypothesising start to impinge on the cloistered calm of scholarship, the situation can be headed off simply with a shrug and a sigh (where the general public are concerned) or fury and ostracism (if a fellow-professional should find himself involved). These strategies are wholly successful in preserving academic disciplines as cosy niches for clever but intellectually unenquiring people. Long holidays too.

None of this need concern us; we are neither hierophants nor laity, so let us browse among the anomalies and decide for ourselves whether they point to the Early History of Britain being fact or fiction.

Anomaly One: Changing Everyone's Language

Early British history is for the most part much like early history anywhere in the world: essentially the account of a particular people, speaking a particular language, periodically being invaded by foreigners speaking a different language. The invading foreigners set up their own state with themselves as a political elite, speaking in their own language, while the native population continues to speak in *their* own language. In the fullness of time each set of invaders must do one of, or a combination of, four things:

1. Leave – as, for example, the Romans left Britain in the 5th century AD.

2. Be supplanted by other invaders – as, for example, the Anglo-Saxons were by the Normans in the 11th century.

3. Get merged into the native population – as, for example, the Danes were in northern and midland England.

4. Replace the native population on a permanent basis – as, for example, the English-speakers did in North America.

In the first three cases it's the language of the invaders that disappears, in the fourth it's the native language that disappears. Since it's an 'observable fact' in the case of the British Isles that the language allegedly introduced by the Anglo-Saxons (English) is overwhelmingly dominant except in limited areas to the north and west where Celtic languages (Welsh, Scots Gaelic and Irish) are spoken, it follows – according to orthodoxy – that the Anglo-Saxons must have 'replaced' the Celtic-speakers (except in the north and west), or at the very least put in place circumstances that led the natives to switch over en masse from their native tongue to that of their new rulers. On the face of things, this demands an explanation, because:

1. The usual British pattern – followed by the Belgae, the Romans, the Danes, the Norwegians and the Normans – is that the invaders set up a governing *apparat* and leave the inhabitants much as they always were.

2. 'Persuading' the natives to speak the invaders' language normally happens when the invaders are culturally in advance of the natives, whereas the Anglo-Saxons were culturally far in arrears of the Romanised Celtic Britons.

3. 'Removing' the natives normally requires either that the two populations be so genetically isolated that infectious diseases more or less do the work irrespective of any overt action on the part of the invaders, or that the native population is small and the incoming population is large. Neither applies in the case of the Anglo-Saxons and the Celtic Britons.

So, it seems, the Anglo-Saxons were both unusual in British history in replacing the native population (or at any rate their language) and unusual in not having an obvious means of carrying out this radical step. And of course it's faintly bewildering why they should want to do so, since normally a ruling class needs a large underclass that is easily distinguishable from itself. But one might say that *being unusual* does not constitute *an anomaly*. What makes the Anglo-Saxons unusually unusual is that they were not merely unique in the annals of

British history but, apparently, unique in contemporary Western European history too. Here is a list of the various barbarian tribes who occupied Western Europe after the collapse of the Roman Empire and the effect they had on the local population, judged by whether the local language situation was altered by the invaders:

(a) **Western European countries within the Roman Empire**	(b) **Subsequently occupied by**	(c) **Was language of (a) changed to that of (b)?**
Portugal	Visigoths	No
	Vandals	No
	Arabs	No
Spain	Visigoths	No
	Vandals	No
	Arabs	No
France	Visigoths	No
	Vandals	No
	Burgundians	No
	Franks	No
	Normans	No
Britain	**Anglo-Saxons**	**Yes**
	Danes	No
	Normans	No
Italy	Visigoths	No
	Vandals	No
	Ostrogoths	No
	Lombards	No
	Normans	No

Anomalous? We'd probably call it ludicrous, but that's not what is most interesting to an Applied Epistemologist. It's the fact that you will not find this table, or anything like it, or anything that even alludes to the general problem, anywhere 'in the literature'. Not a dicky. Now this is a quite different scale of epistemological phenomenon from mere incompetence. It's just about acceptable for historians to say, 'OK, so the Anglo-Saxons did something nobody else managed and we don't know why', but it's unconscionable for them to say nothing about it whatsoever. Do they even know? Well, that's one of the things about cognitive dissonance … they do and they don't. It's not that historians are exactly ignorant of the anomaly – everything in the table is perfectly familiar to any Western European historian – it's that they are *carefully unconcerned*. If you showed this table to any tenured historian in any British university, he would first evince ignorance, in the sense of unfamiliarity; then he would mount some pedantic objection to something or other in the table, then finally he would say, 'So what?' Always be wary of people who say 'So what?' to a complex problem they have never thought about before.

Of course, the 'so what' in this case is that the Anglo-Saxons happen to be the chief component of the British Creation Myth, that the present inhabitants of Britain are held to be the descendants of these Anglo-Saxons and the language that modern-day Britons speak is held to be a modern form of the Anglo-Saxon language. So if none of this is true, and Anglo-Saxon is actually a Germanic language related to but distinct from English and spoken only by a foreign military caste that happened to rule England for a few hundred years, then the whole British Creation Myth is in deep trouble. And with it the foundations of all British history. But this book has a wider purpose than the mere correction of the beliefs held by the inhabitants of some dim offshore island. You should, throughout this book, be asking yourself why the blindingly obvious things outlined here from time to time are so studiously ignored by professional historians and, having come to the conclusion that this is a moderately scandalous situation, you should then apply these thoughts to academics and academia in general. And rise up and kick the rascals out. Or at any rate formulate the view that if the most highly educated of us are capable of such folly, it doesn't say much for what passes for thought amongst everybody else. This will in turn allow you to question the universally-held nostrum that education is a self-evidently good thing and that it should therefore expand exponentially. Then, finally, you will be able to consider the proposition that cultures (and individuals) are most successful – including intellectually successful – when education has to be striven for in exactly the same way as are all other goods and services; that compulsory education is – save possibly for the inculcation of the three R's – a waste of time and money; and that freely-available higher education produces only highly-educated fools. When you've worked it all out, let me know the answer, as I am somewhat highly educated myself.

Anomaly Two: The Celtic Fringe

The presumably Anglo-Saxon writers of the *Anglo-Saxon Chronicle* distinguish between the 'British' and the 'Welsh', reserving the term 'English' for themselves. This is puzzling because, according to the usual account, everybody in England and Wales was speaking the same language – an early form of Welsh – when the Romans arrived in the 1st century AD, and for the next 400 years everybody in England and Wales lived in a unitary political state (the Roman Empire) and continued to speak that common language (plus Latin). How then, in the short interval between the Romans leaving and the Anglo-Saxons setting up their states, could the 'British' have organised themselves into a single people and the Welsh have organised *themselves* into a different people? The short answer, I suppose, would have to be 'they couldn't', which would in turn mean that this distinction must have existed before the Romans arrived. So either 'British' is an unknown language spoken throughout non-Welsh Britain which has disconcertingly disappeared, or 'British' is simply English and nothing and nobody has disappeared. Everybody is speaking the same language in the same places in recorded times as they were in unrecorded times.

This is a problem that bedevils the whole of ancient history, because 'history' is defined as the sum of contemporary sources – but contemporary sources in ancient times tended neither to know nor to care about the intricacies of local linguistics. The *recorders* of history were, virtually by definition, the makers of history, since literate groups tended overwhelmingly to dominate illiterate ones. So, for instance, one might be reading an engrossing account of Carthaginians versus Greeks in Sicily when suddenly Polybius (or whoever) will make passing reference to the Siciliots living in the hinterland who are neither Greek nor Carthaginian. And one is suddenly reminded that the Greeks and the Carthaginians are just a bunch of Johnny-come-latelies who occupied a few coastal towns and that 'Sicily' must actually be largely populated by Siciliots, speaking 'Sicilian', irrespective of who actually controlled the island politically.

Ancient historians tend to write exclusively about 'the warring classes'. When Caesar takes on 'the Gauls', we can't tell whether this is a just a case of a new bunch of invaders taking on the previous bunch of invaders or whether the Romans are fighting the aboriginal inhabitants. Of course, the common people do get mentioned in law codes, but unfortunately here again they get short shrift by being referred to generically as serfs, helots, slaves, villeins, rustics and other linguistically unhelpful terms. The only early historian who appears to make an effort at sorting out the language groups is the Venerable Bede, but unfortunately the passage in which he lists the peoples of Britain would seem to be a later interpolation. Indeed, the interpolation might be from as late as the Tudor period when, alas, the Anglo-Saxon = English assumption was already firmly established. It's one of the curiosities of the study of history that early errors are given greater weight than later ones, since there's a general presumption that early=authentic.

Oftentimes, the best we can do is to adopt a scheme that makes sense. This generally turns out to be by using the Applied Epistemological principle, '*What is* is *what was* – unless you've got bone-chilling evidence to the contrary.' In the case of vernacular languages, this permits us to see under the historical account – which is a story of much comings-and-goings by various invading foreign-speakers – to the substrate of ordinary inhabitants who carry on century after century, indeed millennium after millennium, occupying the same land which they till for whomsoever happens to be the ruling class. This accords both with our modern knowledge and of course common sense, since no invading foreign-speaking elite would rid their newly-won territory of the very element that gives it value. But orthodoxy appears to follow a different principle: 'If *what is* is really *what was*, then we don't have very much of a story to tell, so let's go with something a whole lot more exciting and hang the consequences.' And certainly the orthodox tale is highly spiced. The present Celtic Fringe, we are assured, came about because the whole of the British Isles was once Celtic-speaking until the Anglo-Saxons came along and started an extraordinary campaign of ethnic cleansing so that in double-quick time the Celtic-speakers had been driven out to the furthest reaches of England, Wales and Scotland.

These Celtic rumps keep on turning up, irrespective of who is impinging on whom, but always and everywhere possessing their unique language despite having apparently being driven into their little corners quite recently. But the really weird thing is that the dominant language group can always expunge them from virtually the whole of the mainland but can *never* quite finish the job. Hence in Scotland, the Scottish Lallan-speakers (i.e. English-speakers) can effortlessly displace the Celtic-speakers until they get to the highlands and islands, where all of a sudden they can't; in Wales the Anglo-Saxons can't get past Offa's Dyke, the Normans can't get past the marcher lands and the modern English, despite seven centuries of absolute control, have had to give up on monolingualism and give the natives Channel 4C; in Ireland the Celts are still out there on the western boonies; in England everybody got converted in no time flat, except for the Cornish who lasted until the end of the 18th century; in France the Romans couldn't get the Bretons to give up their language; and in Spain the Celtiberians in the north-east corner hung on we know not how long. (And don't mention the Basques, who seem to survive everything everybody throws at them without breaking sweat.)

So you've got a choice between:

1. The *Orthodox Account*. In six different countries the locals were forced to change their language quite suddenly by three different sets of invaders, but each set of invaders was entirely unable to persuade a sliver of locals along the western seaboard from changing their language.

2. The *Applied Epistemological Account*. Nobody was forced to change anything because everyone is speaking the language they always did. The only event of note is that a bunch of Celtic-speakers (plus some Basques) showed up and successfully colonised the western seaboard of Europe.

And the winner is ... One of the great principles of Applied Epistemology is: 'The truth tends to be a bit boring.' That's because of Occam's Razor, which states that we should choose the argument that makes the fewest unnecessary assumptions. This enjoins simplicity on all arguments, and simplicity makes for dull history. At any rate, it does at first. Once based on true foundations, history tends to flourish rather magnificently. But that's in the long run; in the short run, professional practitioners have lecture time to fill and books to write, so we get a picture of restless movement and constant change. Languages appear and disappear with giddy speed right up until the days of mass literacy when the written record at last reflects the language that everybody actually speaks. Then nobody seems to change their language. Weird. Bear this in mind as we wend our way through the history of the British Isles because, not surprisingly, given the sheer unlikelihood of the orthodox scenario, each discrete part of the Celtic Fringe has its very own sub-set of anomalies.

Cornwall

The Anglo-Saxons conquered and ruled Cornwall in much the same way, and only a little after, they conquered the rest of England; but for some unaccountable reason they omitted to 'replace' the Cornish, who continued to speak their native Celtic language until it finally died out at the end of the 18th century. So, it seems, for more than a thousand years Cornwall managed to retain a language that was expunged completely and rapidly everywhere else in England. Again, is this just a one-off, unusual occurrence that history has thrown up, or is it an anomaly that points to the whole basic assumption being wrong? It's true, of course, that Cornwall is a 'one-off' corner of England and is thereby definitely a candidate for the old 'that's just the way it happened' explanation so beloved of orthodoxy, but of course Cornwall is just one of six examples of 'long-term Celtic survival', so one might say 'it just happened six different ways in six different places'. And Cornwall wasn't the far-off fustian corner we know today – thanks to the tin trade, it was plugged right into the mainstream of British and Continental life.

But still, let's assume our schoolbooks have got it right and dear old Anglo-Saxon clanked its way across Celtic England. Since the Anglo-Saxons achieved complete political dominance over the whole of England by the 7th century AD but had lost that dominance over half of England by the 10th century and were ousted entirely shortly thereafter, this means they had 300 years or so to alter the language of England from 100 per cent Celtic to 100 per cent Anglo-Saxon. But all this happened during the Dark Age when we can't know what was really going on, whereas in Cornwall the changeover occurred in the bright day of modern history ... so we do know what happened. We know precisely when the Anglo-Saxons arrived in Cornwall (7th century) and we know precisely when Cornish finally disappeared (18th century). So we have a definite known example to use in judging the hypothetical case. How do they compare? Well, if we applied the Cornish experience (Anglo-Saxon taking a thousand years to expunge Cornish, i.e. to move less than a hundred miles) to the hypothetical English one, we would get a timetable something like:

Hengist and Horsa arrive on the Kent coast in 495 AD;

London would by now in 2006 be thoroughly English-speaking;

Buckinghamshire would be half-and-half;

Birmingham still entirely Celtic-speaking.

Mmm ... something wrong there.

Scotland

The Scots are a great pre-historical puzzle. It's not even clear when they ceased to be pre-historical because Hadrian's Wall (dividing England from Scotland) was mostly the official boundary between Civilisation and Barbarism, but the Antonine Wall (where Glasgow and Edinburgh are today) was in use for part of the Roman occupation of Britain, and in any case fixed Roman defensive boundaries were never in themselves the limit of Roman civilising influences. Roman and other sources are very unenlightening about the language situation in Scotland, except that it would appear that, in the far north, there was a rather fierce people speaking Pictish – a language still indecipherable today – but other than that, the Roman (and the archaeological) evidence seems to lump everybody else together, north and south of the border. So what *were* the locals speaking at the time?

Let's consider an ordinary everyday community of people living in c. 0 BC somewhere in the middle of what we would nowadays call the Scottish borders, that is, between where the Hadrian and Antonine walls would later be built. To preserve strict objectivity, let's assume only that they are speaking Language X, about which we have no information. These X-speakers first enter history, i.e. the written record, when the Romans arrive in the 1st century AD and – in the 2nd century – build Hadrian's Wall immediately to the south of them. Does this affect them? It would doubtless make cattle raiding more difficult, but we know from better recorded areas of Roman *limes* – lines of defence along the borders of the Empire – on the Rhine and Danube that the general trend would be for the Roman garrisons on the wall, and the towns that grew up around them, to provide a local outlet for agricultural surpluses, trade, military recruitment, an array of low-level interchange between the not-yet-very-civilised south and the even-less-civilised north.

So far as language is concerned, these interchanges would certainly require the development of some kind of lingua franca and, fortunately, there already was a local lingua franca

– Language X – because it's another safe assumption that the people living south of Hadrian's Wall (not a geographical barrier) would also be Language X-speakers and, they being *inside* the Roman Empire, would have no shortage of bilingual Latin/Language X-speakers.

What happens when the Antonine Wall is built and our Scottish X-speakers become formally incorporated within the Empire? Nothing very much, since the archaeological evidence is perfectly clear, from its paucity of Roman material, that this was a marcher region, of military rather than of cultural or economic significance. It's doubtful if the ordinary inhabitants of Galashiels or Peebles or Lockerbie (whatever they were called then) would very often hear Latin spoken, much less learn to speak it themselves. Nevertheless, Latin *would* make some inroads: the local administrative class would no doubt learn Classical Latin; some men would join the army and learn Soldier's (or Dog) Latin; some women would become camp-followers and also learn Dog Latin and, it's not unreasonable to suppose, their children might habitually speak Dog Latin, at any rate bilingually with Language X.

Even so, common sense tells us that none of this would impinge greatly on the population in general and, with the Roman withdrawal from the Antonine Wall after scarcely a hundred years, Latin would cease to make further inroads. The complete departure of the Legions from Britain in the 5th century would presumably lead to Latin ceasing to exist anywhere in southern Scotland, save perhaps for the purposes of writing (X being an unwritten language). This is all entirely orthodox. We can be confident that 5th-century lowland Scots would still be speaking Language X.

The next thing we know about southern Scotland from historical sources is that Irish invaders set up states in the western half (Dalriada and Strathclyde) and Anglo-Saxon invaders set up states in the east (Berenicia and Northumbria). How would this have affected Language X? We have no specific information, but we do know in a general kind of way that Dark Age Scottish statecraft didn't approach Roman levels of cultural penetration, so it's a reasonable surmise that if Latin didn't replace the local language, it's hard to imagine either Irish or Anglo-Saxon doing so. The same holds true for any of the other waves of invaders – Welsh, Norwegians, Danes, highland Gaels and Normans – that affected lowland Scotland from time to time. The only question that arises is whether the local population, the Language X-speakers, continued living there through all these vicissitudes. Here again we can't know for certain, but since southern Scotland isn't the kind of prime real estate attractive to incomers en masse, but rather the kind of marginal land that can be worked only on a *latifundia* or large estate basis – that is, an economic system relying entirely on a pliable workforce – any invading group would have been positively perverse to get rid of the locals.

Nevertheless, the Official Scottish Creation Myth requires that one group, *but only one group*, of invaders did this very thing: the Anglo-Saxons. Since the creation myth insists that the medieval population of the Scottish lowlands spoke a modern version of Anglo-Saxon – that is, 'Lallan Scots', the northernmost dialect of English – it follows that these incoming Anglo-Saxons either physically replaced the X-speakers or, at the very least, forced them to switch languages. But why the Anglo-Saxons and none of the others? Not, it would seem, for any of the reasons that might, by a stretch of the imagination, account for this remarkable makeover:

1. The Anglo-Saxons weren't there very long (they arrived in Scotland late and were replaced by other groups quite quickly).

2. The Anglo-Saxons weren't particularly ubiquitous (they appear to have stuck close to the eastern coastline and never spread further than the south-eastern corner of Scotland).

3. They didn't introduce a written language (by then the locals already had access to two written languages, Latin and Irish).

4. They didn't introduce a new religion (it was the Anglo-Saxons that got converted).

5. There weren't very many of them (the Scottish Anglo-Saxons appear to have been an expeditionary force of an expeditionary force).

In fact the *sole* reason why it's assumed that the Anglo-Saxons *must have done so* is because when we have unequivocal historical evidence about what the ordinary natives were actually speaking – that is, when Scottish vernacular poetry and prose began to be written down in the late medieval period – it turns out that everybody was speaking English. Or *Scots* as the medieval Scots understandably called what appeared to them to be their own language, though nowadays they, like the rest of Britain, and the rest of the world, have adopted the South

Midland version of this language. And since it's a 'well-known historical fact' that English is an evolved version of Anglo-Saxon, it follows that *Scots* must have come from the same source.

An innocent in creation myth mythology might suppose that Scottish historians would be only too pleased to be able to claim that this *Scots* is in fact Language X, since it would thereby give them a wonderfully long lineage and proof positive that they can survive anything thrown at them by invaders – a very potent myth for small nations. However, this was not to be; the Scots are particularly proud of their educational status, so they tend to be especially in thrall to academic paradigms. Or, to put it another way, Scottish historians are a subject-people of English historians and are thus obliged to accept on trust all English historical paradigms, one of which insists *as an absolute fact* that English is derived from Anglo-Saxon. They are therefore duty bound by the rigours of academic discipline to accept that the Scots must have got their variety of English from the same source. (Though, just as typically, as soon as the Scottish intelligentsia had satisfactorily completed the switch from Scots English to Standard English during the Scottish Enlightenment, they hijacked the nascent English dictionary industry, the bedrock of the whole Anglo-Saxon-into-English theory. But that's another story.)

Now that there's a Scottish Parliament again, perhaps the Scots would care to declare linguistic independence. True, this would mean recognising that the Scots and the English have always spoken more or less the same language and therefore must have always been more or less the same people, but, as no doubt they will be quick to point out, there's no reason to suppose that Scotland isn't the original homeland and *Scots* the original language, thereby rendering England a Scottish colony and Standard English a regional dialect of *Scots*. It would also mean the lowland Scots recognising that the highland (i.e. Gaelic-speaking) Scots are a quite different people and that for the good burghers of Edinburgh to wear kilts on Burns Night (and any other excuse the poor mutts get) makes about as much sense as me wearing a kimono on St George's Day.

Ireland

When the entirely English-speaking Gerry Adams addresses an entirely English-speaking Sinn Fein audience in broad Gaelic, one can be reasonably sure that something mythic lurks in the mists of Old Ireland. What *did* the native Irish speak before the English arrived and forced them all to speak English? Unionists and Nationalists are agreed on one thing – the natives were definitely all speaking *Erse*, Irish Gaelic, a firmly Celtic language. Only Applied Epistemologists disagree with this cosy consensus, because the rule '*What is* is *what was*' dictates that Ireland was almost certainly exactly like England, Wales and Scotland: Celtic-speaking in the west, English-speaking in the east. Because there's no bone-chilling evidence to the contrary.

So first, let's deal with the 'historical' evidence. None of it is in English. All early Irish documentation is in either Gaelic or Latin. Is this significant? Not particularly; English wasn't a written language in early Irish times so there couldn't be any English sources, no matter how many English-speakers there were in Ireland. Needless to say, as soon as English was a written language, in the late medieval period, English texts turn up in Ireland. But more seriously, all early Irish people seem to have Gaelic names. Is this significant? Not particularly; everybody in Roman times had a Latin name – it doesn't mean that everybody's mother-tongue was Latin. Names always get transliterated into the language they are being written in. Especially toffs' names. In fact, only toffs ever enter the written record – be it as saints or kings or heroes – and we have reason to suppose that all the toffs in Ireland were Gaelic-speakers wherever they lived. Why so? Well, for a minority language group to exist at all along a particular coastline, they must dominate the hinterland. As soon as they don't, the hinterland majority will simply blow them away. That doesn't necessarily mean they get driven into the sea; it just means that as soon as the barriers are down, the language cline (a line drawn so that a majority of people on one side speak a given language while those on the other side speak another) will move rapidly in favour of the majority group. Every time there's a mixed marriage, the kids adopt the more useful language; and unless the coastal minority have some clear politico-cultural advantage, that language is always the majority language.

For instance, the Arab-speakers along the North African coast are still there because, by and large, they have maintained their ascendancy over the inland non-Arab tribes. But the Celts themselves demonstrate what happens when they become 'just a linguistic minority'. As soon as English-speakers achieved political dominance in England, Scotland and Wales in the late medieval period (in England after King John lost Normandy in the early 13th century, in Wales under Edward I later the same century, and in Scotland at some undetermined earlier *Macbeth*ian time when the various Anglo-Saxon, Gaelic and Viking rulers were no more), the Cornish, the Welsh, the Cumbrians and the Scots Gaels were on the back foot. Ditto France and Spain. Ditto Ireland. So in earlier times we can be pretty sure that the Celts were top-dogs in Britain, Ireland, France and Spain. Boadicea might have been a Celt (though even that is not knowable), her army might have been Celtic, but your actual peasantry were almost certainly English-speakers. If we assume that the same applied in eastern Ireland – that is, an aboriginal population of English-speakers with a thin upper crust of Celtic-speakers – then we would have a situation entirely consistent with the historical sources: the historical personages (not to mention the writers of historical documentation) would be wholly Celtic and the records themselves would be written in either Latin or Gaelic. (Irish was a written language centuries before English was.)

Nonetheless, this is all speculation. We have no actual evidence that eastern Ireland was English-speaking. The most we can say is that it's an open question, one that has to be addressed by deciding whichever version makes the most sense. So let's see which version that is. How does orthodoxy account for the fact that the *present* people of Ireland speak English, apart of course from the usual Celtic fringe out on the western littoral? Irish historians, not notably subject to English historical paradigms, take up the story (in bold):

1. **Strongbow invades in the 12th century and introduces the Irish to life under the English yoke, etc.**
   True, but anomalous, because Strongbow and the entire

leadership were French-speaking Normans, the rank-and-file were either Dutch-speaking Flemings or Welsh-speaking Welshmen and the government they formally answered to (in Latin) was the French-speaking one then ruling in London. It's doubtful if anybody in the entire party could have spoken English even if they had wanted to. The puzzle is not how the Irish managed to learn to speak English under the Norman yoke, but how the Normans managed to learn to speak English when in Ireland. Unless the Irish were *already* speaking English and the Normans just went native as they did in Normandy, England, Scotland, Calabria, Sicily and Greece.

2. **In later medieval times, the English – that is, the real English-speaking English – set up a government in Dublin, and English became the normal language in the 'Pale', a loosely defined area extending for about 50 or 100 miles in all directions from Dublin, and outside which ('beyond the Pale') lay 'Irish' Ireland.** True, but anomalous, because the English were not colonists in the modern sense of promoting settlement by English-speakers at the expense of the natives, they were normal workaday medieval dynastic magnates holding foreign territory by force. It is, on the face of things, as surprising to find a large English-speaking area around Dublin as it would be to find large English-speaking areas around Bordeaux or Calais, districts similarly occupied by the English for many centuries on the same basis. Yes, we would expect

the usual practices of anglification within the upper classes and bilingual couplings lower down the social order, but we have no reason to suppose that Irish-speakers were any less wedded to their mother-tongue than were their French-speaking contemporaries. If, on the other hand, Ireland was indeed Celtic-speaking in the west, English-speaking in the east, then we would have a situation exactly like the Pale.

3. **In the 16th century, the English government did start a policy of outright colonisation, with the Ulster plantations.** True, but anomalous, because from then until now the English immigrant-colonists – in practice mostly English-speaking Scots – have pursued the most vigorous anti-native policies and yet, to this day, after 400 years of unremitting imperialism (from the world champions of imperialism), the natives have managed, without obvious difficulty, not merely to survive but to retain all their badges of cultural identity. Except apparently the most important one of all, their language. Unless it was their language.

All in all, one would have to say that the revisionist version works best. Though whether the Irish will take kindly to having their north–south splittist assumptions replaced by east–west ones is pretty doubtful. The Irish, like everyone else, learn nothing and forget nothing.

Wales

Wales is the greatest Celtic anomaly of all, or rather the smallest. For reasons which unfold later in the book, the label

'Celtic' has become a default mode – whenever a particular area has an unknown language, academic specialists are constitutionally averse to sticking the label 'Unknown' on the map, so they put in the default language. What seems to happen is that in the early days of a subject, a model is proposed so that, for instance, the ancient linguistic map of Europe has bits that are known ('Latin', 'Greek', 'Punic') plus some conjectures ('Celtic', Scythian', 'Germanic'). This then gets taught to students quite properly as a proposed model, and these students when they grow up to be academics of their own start to refine the model, again perfectly properly, so that each label becomes a mite more sophisticated. Hence the bald 'Celtic' starts to transmogrify into Celtiberian, Celtic (P), Celtic (Q), Eastern Celtic, etc., and these in turn start to turn up on the linguistic maps. Gradually, as generations pass and each band of undergraduates dutifully writes up its lecture notes from lecturers who are unlikely to be themselves specialists in this area, it is forgotten that still, even now, we do not have a single unequivocal example of what any ancient people were speaking. We have evidence as to what some of them were *writing*, plus conjecture, but I doubt if you would be able to find a linguistic map that is other than chock-full of language labels. The word 'Unknown' is still conspicuously absent.

Applied Epistemology, by contrast, just lays the *present* linguistic pattern over a map of Europe and then starts adjusting language boundaries by what is *definitely* known. So, for instance, we know from 19th-century census records that Celtic-speakers in Britain and Ireland were more widespread than they are today, so we shift the cline between English and Celtic in an easterly direction. Do we extrapolate this tendency?

That depends. If we had records of Irish famines, mass emigrations, industrial revolutions – the kind of things that lead to radical cline-change in modern times – then we might; but if we don't, we apply the 'Cornish' model, since that's the only English–Celtic language cline we have good historical evidence for. As far as the Welsh go, we would probably also use place-name evidence as well, since the difference between Welsh names and English names is fairly stark. And we'd finish up with a language boundary running vaguely parallel to, but slightly to the west of, Offa's Dyke. Which is of course essentially the present Wales/England political border. How little do the essentials change over time.

Orthodoxy, of course, takes a decidedly different view. As far as it is concerned, there was originally no language cline since everybody spoke Welsh. Then along came the Anglo-Saxons, who killed off all the Welsh-speakers until their blood-lust became exhausted somewhere along the western Mercian boundary and they built Offa's Dyke to make sure that the Welsh remnant couldn't go in for a bit of ethnic *wirgild* on their own account. Applied Epistemologists would say that the Anglo-Saxons were able to conquer the native English-speakers of Britain without difficulty because English-speakers had always been the local aboriginal underclass; but they couldn't manage the Welsh-speakers because all the Celtic groups were self-conscious ruling elites. The Welsh may not have been as strong as the Anglo-Saxons, but they were strong enough to make it not worth the Anglo-Saxons' while to conquer them. The Normans, who were even stronger, took the same common-sense view. Only when the English had ceased to be an underclass, by the time of Edward I, was the fundamental imbalance between English- and Welsh-speakers reflected in the political geography.

The Welsh have one very great distinction. They are the only viable Celtic language group in the world today. With apologies to the Scots Gaels holding out with some élan in their island fastnesses, the Welsh are all we have left. And from what? According to orthodoxy, Celtic-speakers used to stretch across Europe: the British Isles, Iberia, France, Italy, a slice of the Balkans, Turkey ... So there's a thing – the biggest language group in unrecorded Europe becomes the smallest one in *recorded* Europe. And not a smidgen of evidence to account for how this stupendous change came about! How can anyone believe this tarradiddle?

Certainly it runs counter to everything we know *from direct observation* about the way language clines normally move. In the first place, they mostly don't move very much at all; languages persist with quite extraordinary tenacity so that even today, in the face of the fiercest cultural pressure from the 'majors', quite tiny language groups hang around and even modestly flourish. But in so far as language clines do move, it's true that, left to itself, the cline always acts against the minority language because both in mixed marriages and in population movements from one side to the other, it nearly always pays individuals to learn the majority language, or at least – and perhaps more significantly in the long run – to make sure their children do. But in Britain it was *Celtic* that was the majority language, or so it's alleged. There were millions of native Celtic-speakers, whereas the Anglo-Saxons were numbered in boatloads.

But, argue historians (and Celtic nationalists), things were not 'left to themselves'; it was political dominance that led to language dominance. This is a perfectly acceptable proposition in itself, and there's certainly some merit to the argument in the case of Ireland and Wales, where the English did from time to time espouse a conscious – sometimes a brutal – language policy. But it should be noted that centuries of anglification in Wales seem not to have extinguished Welsh, and decades of political nourishment of Gaelic in the Irish Republic have led only to its speedy extinction. But in Scotland the idea of political dominance promoting linguistic dominance is utterly ludicrous, because the Anglo-Saxons had political dominance for scarcely 200 years and over barely one-tenth of the land area, after which Scotland was unified by a northern (presumed Gaelic-speaking) dynasty and then ruled by Normans in so far as there was any central political dominance in Scotland. With only the most tenuous of political, military, economic or cultural links with England, it passes comprehension that English-speaking would eventually come to dominate Scotland. There's only one circumstance that could lead to such a thing, and that's if English-speaking always dominated Scotland.

But historians are blithely unaware of any of this. They aren't asked to consider the evidence for the paradigm assumptions of their subject; they are taught the paradigms in the first five minutes – or better still are assumed to know them when they arrive – and then they get down to some *proper* history. Naturally enough, this leads to a fair amount of high comedy when the proper history comes up against the paradigm error. Here's a typical example taken from *The Isles – A History*, currently the standard generalist textbook, by Norman Davies, Professor Emeritus at the University of

London, Supernumerary Fellow of Wolfson College, Oxford, Fellow of the British Academy, etc., etc.:

> It is an extraordinary fact that the emerging common language of Britannia's Germanic settlers, which had passed its formative centuries in a predominantly Celtic environment, contained barely a handful of Celtic words. This is seized on by the exterminationists to argue that there were no Celtic mothers around to teach the Celtic vocabulary to the children of mixed marriages. But there may be other explanations. It is hard to believe that the dialects of the illiterate migrants did not make any borrowings from the languages of the partly literate country to which they had come. On the other hand, it is all too easy to believe that at a much later stage those same Germanic educators who were following the norms of Roman Christianity so slavishly would also have favoured linguistic purism and would have purged all Celtic traits from their speech. The early mongrel dialects would never have been recorded. Only the late, purged, and purified language was current when the Germanics finally became literate.

First, a couple of technical points. The Anglo-Saxons were renowned throughout Europe for the barbarousness of their Latin, so their contemporaneous obsession to 'purify' their own language is to be applauded. Nor is it entirely accurate (or indeed at all accurate) to say 'when the Germanics finally became literate' – they were literate in Latin virtually from the start and became literate in Anglo-Saxon very soon thereafter.

These quibbles aside, Professor Davies does conjure up a

very beguiling picture of the later Anglo-Saxons, because purging words from everyday discourse is, as the modern French government could tell him, a very formidable task. To begin with, it would have required the Anglo-Saxons to have invented philological linguistics a thousand years before we thought it had been invented, because even *knowing* that such-and-such a word is of Celtic origin and was incorporated in one's own language 500 years before is a remarkable feat in itself; but to make a *list* of these words in the days before dictionaries and other little props were available is quite magnificent. Still, we can postulate a small group of Anglo-Saxon linguistic zealots (it would have to be small, since there were only ever a few thousand literate Anglo-Saxons to start with, and they had a Church and a State to run between times) getting together, possibly somewhere on the Wessex/Mercia border (Oxford would have been an excellent choice), making the list of all these words with a 'Celtic trait' and then going off into the villages of England to spread the message. Here, they did run into a problem. The villagers of Anglo-Saxon England were wholly illiterate, so our linguistic missionaries would have been obliged to teach them by rote to memorise all the Celtic words in order to ... forget them. A thankless task in the best of circumstances, but what made it that little bit harder is that the whole business would, for the most part, have had to be carried out in conditions of *complete secrecy*, because most English-speakers at the relevant time were living under Danish or Celtic administrations that might well have taken a dim view of Anglo-Saxon linguistic evangelism.

Still, we do know that these unsung Anglo-Saxon heroes must have done a thoroughly good job, because it's a fact that

English, even today, contains hardly a trace of Celtic influence. It's an honour to have such forebears. Makes you proud to be British ... er ... English ... er ... Anglo-Saxon ... er ...

It will not have escaped your notice by now that the orthodox explanation for these Celtic survivals requires a bewildering assortment of models to arrive at the present situation. These are:

1. In England proper, the Anglo-Saxons completely obliterate the largest of all the Celtic populations in a couple of hundred years, permanently and entirely (including, one might add, their place-names).

2. In Cornwall, they have a bit of trouble initially in actually conquering the territory but, having done so, they fail signally for a thousand years to eliminate the Celtic-speakers.

3. In Wales, the Anglo-Saxons get nowhere; the Normans get a bit further; the later English conquer the entire territory but in 700 years fail to extirpate the Celtic-speakers.

4. In Scotland, neither the Anglo-Saxons nor the later English have more than a fleeting effect, and only in the south-east corner. Nevertheless, Celtic-speakers are all but extirpated from the Scottish mainland.

5. In Ireland, most of the east appears to be entirely English-speaking as soon as the English turn up.

In other words, it's a clear case of cobbling together bits of a false paradigm in order to arrive at a necessary outcome. Let's compare this with the Applied Epistemology version based on '*What is* is *what was* unless there's evidence to the contrary', plus a bit of common sense:

1. The British Isles is occupied by English-speakers some time after the end of the Ice Age.

2. Celtic-speakers invade by sea from the west and occupy the whole of the western littoral of both Britain and Ireland. They maintain some sort of suzerainty over the English-speakers (perhaps their distinctive clan system was superior for war-making purposes – later evidence certainly suggests this).

3. The Romans invade. They are quickly able to occupy the English-speaking areas because the English-speakers are an underclass; also the smaller Celtic areas (Cornwall, Wales, Cumbria), but not where there's a large (or perhaps distant) Celtic population (northern Scotland, Ireland).

4. The Anglo-Saxons invade. Not being as organised as the Romans, the Anglo-Saxons are able to conquer only the English-speaking areas. Much greater difficulty with Cornwall and Cumbria; no chance with Celtic Wales, Scotland, Ireland.

5. The Danes, Norwegians, etc. more or less ditto.

6. The Normans more or less ditto.

7. English-speaking governments come to power in England and Scotland. Now that English and Celtic

are finally on a par, the larger group eventually conquers the smaller group in northern Scotland, west Wales and Ireland beyond the Pale.

8. Start of the slow organic shift in the cline between English and Celtic, now that Celtic is no longer a high-caste language, nor English a low-caste one.

9. Hyper-modern times: Highland Clearances in Scotland, Potato Famine in Ireland, Industrial Revolution in Wales, plus mass media, mass education, mass migration, etc., leads to rapid demise of Celtic-speaking areas in Scotland and Ireland and its radical reduction in Wales.

True, both versions are something of a lash-up, but one makes good sense and the other is a bit soppy. But that's not a relevant criterion when one is taught and the other isn't.

Anomaly Three: The (Non-)Morphology of Languages

Anglo-Saxon is known, from its written records, to have changed very little in the 500 years from the 7th century until the 12th century. English is known, from *its* written records, to have changed very little in the 700 years from the 14th century to the 21st century. Yet, during the intervening period of 200 years or so, as Anglo-Saxon 'developed' into English, it apparently managed to change more or less every single word of itself. This remarkable phenomenon is not much noted by historians but is well known to first-year English Literature students at our more traditional universities, who are required to study

1. the Anglo-Saxon epic *Beowulf*, in which virtually every single word is *incomprehensible* except by translation; and

2. the early English poetry of Chaucer and *Piers Plowman*, in which virtually every single word is *comprehensible* except for spelling.

Of course, first-year English Literature students are too callow, perhaps too cowed, to question why they should be required to make an intensive study of *Beowulf*, a story in a foreign language, set in Sweden, whose sole authenticity derives from a manuscript mysteriously uncovered 500 years later in a Tudor library, but since it's the only bit of hard work the poor dears will undertake during undergraduate careers spent reading books and then discussing them (which the rest of us do without demanding a degree for it), they would do well not to make a fuss. Not that their academic mentors would be very sympathetic if they did, because English Literature departments are stuffed ... staffed by people who had to study boring old *Beowulf* in their day and are damned if the next lot are going to have it any easier.

All English Literature students believe 'as a matter of fact' that English is an evolved form of Anglo-Saxon. They do so because this is a historical question, i.e. something they aren't permitted by academic rules to question because 'it's not their field'. Historians, of course, believe the same thing because they have likewise been assured by linguists that it's true, so it's not their field either. Linguists believe it because ... well, they've always believed it and they've got more important things to attend to than checking out the bona fides of some obscure medieval dialect shift. This particular daisy-chain ends up with the *Oxford English Dictionary*, most of whose entries are wrong because its basic etymological assumptions are wrong. According to these scholarly nincompoops, every English word is either from Old English (which is literally true of course, it's just that Old English isn't Anglo-Saxon) or from French or Latin (you'll have to wait to find out why this isn't so).

Still, there is a reason for Applied Epistemologists being able to recognise this while the rest of the educated populace worship at the shrine of the *OED*. It's because the educated populace have a passion for knowing where their words come from – a passion which of course has to be satisfied by academics – but the actual study of the origin of words has some rather terminal structural problems that make this a trifle difficult:

1. Etymological judgements are made overwhelmingly on how similar two words sound. No attempt at any science is employed in this judgement; it comes down to a bunch of people saying "Tis', "Tisn't'. Not surprisingly, it's "Tis' when it supports the prevailing paradigm and "Tisn't' if it disn't.

2. We don't know how any word in any language sounded before 1900, when sound recording devices were invented. Before that, we have some phonetic records for some languages, and various inferences can be drawn by using other methods for written languages, but basically a study based on sound when reconstructing old languages looks to be doomed from the off.

3. The prevailing paradigm is the genealogy of languages as laid down in standard textbooks (the ones that show Anglo-Saxon evolving out of Low German which is the western branch of Indo-European and so forth). These go back to the founding fathers of linguistics, who happen to have been either Britishers of the Raj with a thing about Sanskrit or German Romantic Nationalists with a thing about German. Both sets of souls were Classically trained, so they all had a sub-thing about Latin and Greek. And glory be, it turns out that Sanskrit, German, Latin and Greek are all fantastically important when it comes to selecting ancestor-languages. Despite the fact that *all* the world's languages appear somewhere on these elaborate genealogies, we in fact have no evidence about which came before which *for any language whatsoever* (save for a few modern pidgins). That's why every language-tree diagram that exists in the world today, no matter how eminent its devisers, no matter how unanimous linguists are about its veracity, is in fact completely crackers.

4. The languages we speak today, and can study in detail, haven't been written down for very long and therefore can't be studied in much historical depth.

5. We know almost nothing about how unwritten languages change over time, which of course is far and away most of the time.

6. The advent of printing and widespread literacy came about not long after most modern languages came to be written down, so it's difficult to know what effect these

changes have had on language morphology, as distinct from their 'natural' demotic development.

7. Languages that do have a long written history – Mandarin, Sanskrit, Hebrew, Latin, Ancient Greek, Classical Arabic, etc. – tend to have liturgical and administrative functions that may (or may not) make them characteristic of languages in general.

Fortunately, Applied Epistemological etymologists have their very own principle that cuts through all these difficulties: '*What is* is *what was* unless there's unequivocal evidence that it wasn't.' So we start with the languages that we actually speak and work backwards, rather than make over-educated guesses and work forwards. Although our records about the languages we actually speak go back only a thousand years or so (Irish Gaelic seems to be the earliest, c. the 8th century, French is next, and things gather pace from then on), we do by now have quite a lot of them, so added all together they provide us with an excellent sample for what happens to real, demotic languages over many, many centuries. And that gives us our first rule of thumb: *spoken languages hardly change at all over time.* That's right; if the written language is any guide – and it seems to be a reasonable one – what the (Gaelic) Irish, the French and, inferentially, everyone else were speaking a thousand years ago is recognisably the same as they are speaking today. As we have seen, Anglo-Saxon is no exception to this rule in the sense that, according to its written records, it changes hardly at all for 500 years; and English is no exception either, since, to judge from *its* written record, it hasn't changed radically for 700 years. Which means that Anglo-

Saxon/English, if it's one language, is unique in the entire annals of languages on this our Earth, since it changes every goddamn word of itself.

Obviously, Eng. Lit. Inc. can't take this lying down, but nor would it seem able to fight back very effectively, given the sheer quantity of adverse data. So it has thoroughly muddied the waters. The first thing it did was to invent three different stages of English – Old English, Middle English and Modern English – which fixes in everyone's minds the presumption that while English is a seamless development, it is a radically evolving development. Here's an example of each:

Old English (from Caedmon, c. 8th century):

> Nu scylun hergan hefaenricaes uard,
> metudæs maecti end his modgidanc,
> uerc uuldurfadur, sue he uundra gihuaes,
> eci dryctin, or astelidæ.

Middle English (from Chaucer, *The Prologue*, 14th century):

> A swerd and bokeler bar he by his side …
> A whit cote and a blew hood wered he.
> A bagpipe wel koude he blow and sowne,
> And therwithal he brought us out of towne.

Modern English (from *The Waste Land* by T.S. Eliot, 20th century):

> You cannot say, or guess, for you know only
> A heap of broken images, where the sun beats,
> And the dead tree gives no shelter, the cricket no relief,
> And the dry stone no sound of water.

See, it's seamless but radical: in the first extract you can make out a few English words, in the second even more and in the last all of them. That's true, but it doesn't take an Applied Epistemologist to see that it's also complete bollocks. The first section contains just a handful of words that are the same as, or recognisably the same as, the corresponding English word. But this is true for any passage written in French, German, Dutch, Swedish, Latin, etc. In other words, the first passage is written in a foreign language that happens to be related to English. It doesn't point to Anglo-Saxon as being the precursor of English, indeed the very scarcity of such words is quite good evidence that Anglo-Saxon is *not* a precursor of English. Now take a look at the second passage, but this time we'll ensure that the spelling conventions happen to be the ones you're familiar with. It comes out like this:

A sword and buckler bore he by his side …
A white coat and a blue hood weared he.
A bagpipe well could he blow and sound,
And there with all he brought us out of town.

It's just common-or-garden modern English. The only difference is that the past participle of the verb 'to wear' appears to have changed. That's the sum total of changes in 600 years.

Of course we mustn't be too harsh on the generations of linguists, philologists and etymologists who produced this stuff, much less the busy bees over in the Eng. Lit. and Anglo-Saxon industries who have worked it into such toothsome confections. Every last one of them was intensively instructed on this matter in their first year as undergraduates (by certified experts), given an examination to see if the information had taken firm root (they all passed), lived their entire professional lives among people who believe it to be self-evidently true (who would be turfed out of their professional lives if they didn't), and have never given the matter another thought from that day to this (and, believe me, they're not about to start now). And anyway they're only reacting to English-speakers' desire for a National Creation Myth, and it's an oddity of the human condition that folk would prefer to be descended from a band of *known* Germanic desperadoes than be bereft as uneponymous orphans of the Ice Age.

To be charitable, though, without the peerless assistance of Applied Epistemology there really are technical difficulties in sieving out English from Anglo-Saxon:

1. There's not much primary evidence to go on. After 1066 almost all surviving written records are in either Latin or Norman French; 'native' literature (whether in Anglo-Saxon or 'Middle' English) is quite incredibly scarce. (*Why it's so scarce seems never to detain the experts. According to orthodoxy, an entire country with several centuries' experience of writing down their language suddenly dropped the habit when the Normans came along. Nobody bats an eyelid at this quite astonishing lacuna.*)

2. What has survived is material that is poetic, religious or administrative, i.e. full of archaisms, legalese, loan-words, syntactical extravagancies, bardic formulae and other non-vernacular, non-representative forms. (*Though as we shall see, 'what has survived' isn't quite what it seems.*)

3. Anglo-Saxon and English are undoubtedly closely related

languages, so word-roots are often the same. Once you throw in vagaries of spelling and pronunciation, the scope for mistaken attributive provenances becomes formidable. (*And if you're actively trying to sew the two together, positively overwhelming.*)

4. If they are two separate languages, Anglo-Saxon and English must have existed side by side for many hundreds of years throughout most of Britain, and therefore must have influenced one another to some degree or other. (*On the other hand, Welsh and English have existed side by side for even longer and there are, reputedly, only seven Welsh words in English.*)

5. We have no pure Anglo-Saxon texts to use for comparative purposes, since all Anglo-Saxon texts that have come down to us happen to come from Britain. (*Yes, this isn't the least strange thing about the Anglo-Saxon – England was only an Anglo-Saxon offshoot, yet their continental hoofprint is, for all practical purposes, non-existent.*)

It's not altogether surprising, then, that Anglo-Saxon/English holds (officially) the world record for language change velocity. It's something of which Anglo-Saxonists can be rightly proud, especially as the actual change is recorded in their very own *Anglo-Saxon Chronicle*. For centuries this was written in standard, unchanging Anglo-Saxon (allowing for minor regional variations), but in the 12th century (in its last incarnation written by some Peterborough monks) it suddenly alters and starts to be written in a somewhat garbled, strangulated English, while still using Anglo-Saxon characters. 'Proof positive of rapid language change', say the academics. 'Proof positive of two different languages', say the Applied Epistemologists. To us, it's fairly obvious what the sequence of events was:

Pre-1066 The Anglo-Saxons rule England; Anglo-Saxon monks in the Anglo-Saxon State Church write up the yearly annals in Anglo-Saxon.

1066–c. 1120 The Normans overthrow the Anglo-Saxons. Anglo-Saxon-trained monks continue to write up the yearly annals in Anglo-Saxon, but no further training in Anglo-Saxon is given in the now Norman State Church.

c. 1120 All Anglo-Saxon monks have by now died, retired, etc., and there's nobody left to write up the *Anglo-Saxon Chronicle*.

c. 1120 and after There are, however, English-speaking monks who rather naturally feel that such an anciently established work should be continued. Since they don't speak Anglo-Saxon, they perforce continue it in their own language; but since their own language isn't yet a written one, they transcribe it as best they can using Anglo-Saxon characters.

This is of course why England 'suddenly became illiterate' in 1066. The population had always been illiterate in the sense of speaking an unwritten language. The ruling class, including no doubt inducted English-speakers, were obliged to write in either Anglo-Saxon and Latin or, later, in French and Latin simply because these were the only written languages available to them. Only in late medieval times did English become a written language and hence could the ordinary population write in their own language.

While we're on the subject of rapid change, some attention should be paid to British names. Not place-names, the extravagancies of which we shall excoriate later, but personal names. Named individuals in early historical sources are almost invariably Great Men whose names tend to be both uncharacteristic in themselves and transliterated into whatever language the written record happens to be in at the time. Knowing that Boadicea (a Great Woman, of course) or Agricola or Arthorius or Hengist or the Venerable Bede or Sveyn Bloodaxe or Harold Godwinson or Bishop Odo or Simon de Montfort or William of Orange or George I or Sven-Goran Eriksson lived in Britain tells us little about what language the ordinary inhabitants spoke. 'Ordinary inhabitants' enter history, and under their rightful names, only when vernacular literature and detailed tax records become available, which in Britain didn't occur until the 14th century. At which point, curiously, said records indicate that the vast majority of people living in Britain had names familiar to, indeed largely identical to, 21st-century Britons but not at all like their forebears in the historical record. The orthodox explanation for this state of affairs is that Britons received these names only because they needed to be identified for tax purposes in the 14th century, which is either very true or very circular, but either way we now have another amazing artefact created by 'official history': for the first 1,300 years or so, the inhabitants of Britain changed their names with thrilling rapidity, then c. 1300 they all adopted a quite new set of names, and for the next 700 years didn't change them at all.

It's not specially germane to the overall thesis of this book, but one can't resist mentioning the most egregious *scandale* in this general neck of the academic woods. The name *Beowulf* is one to conjure with – his name is conjured quite a lot in Anglo-Saxon studies because, to a great extent, *Beowulf is* Anglo-Saxon studies. Without *Beowulf*, Anglo-Saxon isn't a 'study' at all, it's a period in English history on a par with Norman England or the Tudors and Stuarts. But chuck in *Beowulf* (and Caedmon and a few other poem fragments) and all of a sudden you've got a language and a literature, and hence it's on a par with the English Department or an honours degree in French. The only tiny flaw in this prospectus is that *Beowulf* (and Caedmon and various other poem fragments) aren't Anglo-Saxon at all. They're modern forgeries. Their only connection with Anglo-Saxon is that a bunch of 16th-century chancers, knowing there was a big market for ye olde parchments, realised that Anglo-Saxon literature would not only sell well in its own right but be virtually immune to amateur antiquarian investigation.

This isn't the view of the Bodleian or the British Museum or half a dozen other proud repositories who confidently believe that their priceless manuscripts are actual Anglo-Saxon compositions written by actual Anglo-Saxons in the 8th, 9th, 10th, 11th or 12th centuries. Indeed, they mount constant symposia to discuss which poem comes from which century, but for some reason that eludes them they can never quite pin anything down ('More research needed!'). It's true, they acknowledge, that for some quite extraordinary and unfathomable reason, all these wondrous poems disappeared utterly without trace for 500 years and then popped up again mysteriously without provenance in Tudor gentry libraries – just at the moment when the English gentry were, post the Reformation, looking around for something to replace all the Catholic material they could no longer collect and proudly display, and just at the moment when there were, post the Dissolution of the Monasteries, a bunch of unemployed ex-monks who happened to be past-masters in the production of ancient charters, fragments of the True Cross and suchlike to order. And oddly, they were the only people in the world at the time with any familiarity whatsoever with Anglo-Saxon.

The only question that remains to be answered is: 'How could a 16th-century forger come up with a masterpiece like *Beowulf*?' One might, I suppose, point out that impoverished poets too were thick on the ground in Tudor England, but a better argument would be that *Beowulf* is not in fact a master-piece. It is *sui generis*, a bit like Homer or the Old Testament, and when assessing such works it's virtually impossible to know what is a masterpiece and what is a thing of wonder only because of its antiqueness and uniqueness. And it would be fair to say that while *The Iliad* or The Song of Solomon sur-vived precisely because they *were* masterpieces, *Beowulf* was clearly a different sort of masterpiece, the sort that nobody thought to mention either in Anglo-Saxon times or for 500 years afterwards. Although when it turned out to be the earliest epic in the 'English' language, everybody in the 20th century queued up to sing its praises. But I'm a Philistine in these matters, so I'll leave it there. Which is alas what the Bodleian, the BM et al. have decided to do likewise: they leave all these priceless 'Anglo-Saxon' documents firmly under lock and key, since one decent carbon dating would blow the whole gaff out of the water. Possibly they know something we don't know. Or perhaps they don't know something we do know.

Anomaly Four: Where the Hell is Everyone?

Historically, human settlement patterns have always fallen into two broad types: in areas where intensive agriculture isn't possible, where pastoralism and crofting are all that local conditions allow, population density is low and people live in isolated houses or widely scattered hamlets. By contrast, in areas of intensive agriculture, population is dense and there's a village every few miles – a distance dictated by the time it takes to walk to the surrounding fields and do a day's work. There is also, typically, a market town every ten-to-twenty miles – again, a distance dictated by the need to get there and back in a day. In addition, there may be larger (and larger) administrative-cum-military centres at even wider intervals depending on the nature of the contemporary state. We know of no society in history (or geography) that breaks this over-whelmingly common-sense arrangement. Except, as usual, Ancient Britain.

Britain is one of the most archaeologically raked-over bits of the Earth's surface, and we know from this archaeology that lowland Britain in the immediate pre-Roman and Roman period was densely populated. As far back as the building of Stonehenge, we can infer that a large local population must have been present, and later on Classical sources confirm that this was so. But throughout lowland Britain there's an eerie lack of evidence as to where all these people were actually living. Individual habitations do turn up from time to time, but no villages and no towns have ever been found. The towns appear in Roman times and the villages are ascribed to Anglo-Saxon foundations. They have to be, because they've all got 'English' names and as we all know, English arrived only with the Anglo-Saxons.

This, then, is the problem: there are (presumably) several million people living in (presumably) several thousand villages for (presumably) several thousand years, and they are all unaccounted for. This 'missing link' has hung around British archaeology for the entirety of its existence and has led to some interesting developments. At first, archaeologists were fond of constructing theories about how low-lying areas were more or less uninhabitable in pre-historic times because the soil was too heavy for the ploughs then in use, whereas high ground was more favourable than it is today because of different climatic conditions. But since this general supposition flies against what is found in all other times in human history and in all other parts of the world, where heavy riverine soils are always a positive population magnet whatever the local climatic conditions, this general thesis has lost some of its allure. Though it can still be found in the more routine textbooks.

Next, the notion was advanced that 'Celtic' people, as a culture, preferred living in isolated houses and widely scattered hamlets. In fact it's even known as the *Celtic field pattern* – small fields usually surrounded by dry-stone walls – and even today you can see it in Cornwall, in Cumbria, in northern Scotland, in Wales, in the west of Ireland. But hold up! Isn't that where the Celts live today? Some coincidence that. But not according to orthodoxy, which believes that the Celts occupied the whole of the British Isles and built these tiddly field systems all over the shop – highlands, lowlands, good soil or bad. Of course, if they knew anything about agriculture they would know instantly that this is rubbish. Nobody in their right mind would ever voluntarily go in for the Celtic field-system because building dry-stone walls around small fields is absolutely back-breaking. The only time you do it is when you have to do it, i.e. in hilly places where the thin soil would soon run off unless you built small fields with substantial breaks. (Actually, it's our equivalent of the even more back-breaking technique of terracing, which is worthwhile only when the local climate gives you two and three crops a year.)

Orthodoxy naturally has to assume that for some unexplained reason the Celtic field-system used to exist in lowland England but has disappeared without trace in the meanwhile, though it's happy enough to acknowledge ordinary large arable fields whenever there's a Roman villa in the vicinity, so it can say: 'Ah-ha, the Romans clearly grubbed up the small fields here and taught the locals how to farm properly.' But for most of England, pre-historians are held in a particularly vicious vice: to farm using ordinary large arable open fields, you need villages; and because all the villages in England have English names, and because the Anglo-Saxons introduced English to England, then the open field system itself has to have been introduced by the Anglo-Saxons. That's the way a false paradigm assumption works, as a will-o'-the-wisp that takes the unwary further and further into the mire.

Then somebody came up with a truly bright idea: yes, the lowland Ancient Brits probably did live in villages and towns just like everybody else in the intensively-farmed world, but … they were unusually fond of building with wood, wattle-

and-daub and other perishable materials (that perished in the boggy lowlands that were so difficult to plough), and hence we could not, nor would ever be able to, *find the evidence*. This argument is so circular that it has taken firm root. Indeed, building these wooden structures and even living in them has become a minor, um, cottage industry amongst the archaeological crowd. Meanwhile, in the real world, a great many 'high-status dwellings' were turning up all over the place, or at any rate their post-holes were. In archaeology-speak, 'high-status dwelling' has largely taken over from 'probably for ritual purposes' as the explanation for anything bigger than a house, making Ancient Britain one of the few places outside the Hollywood Hills where high-status dwellings outnumber ordinary homes. But never mind, because these 'high-status dwellings' have finally solved the problem of where everybody was living. They were living in the high-status dwellings! Of course that's not exactly how it's put, but were you to ask in what were the Ancient Brits living, you would be told 'longhouses', 'communal round-houses', 'Roman villae', whatever the high-status dwelling was called, depending on the period. A beguiling picture of Ancient Britain as a sort of collocation of hippy communes. No wonder the Anglo-Saxons killed them off.

But thank God they did, because now, at last, with the arrival of the Anglo-Saxons we have a complete and continuous archaeological and historical record from then until now. All the history books agree that the Anglo-Saxons, with their heavy ploughs and their village-building skills, were able to get rid of the wretched Celtic system of small-fields-and-isolated-hamlets-and/or-communal-dwellings and set up conventional intensive agriculture, with open field systems and everybody living in proper family-sized houses grouped together in proper village-sized settlements with real honest-to-goodness market towns scattered hither and yon. In short, *Merrie England* had arrived. There's only one objection to this, and unfortunately it's the Anglo-Saxons themselves. They came from southern Scandinavia and eastern Germany where, according to both Ancient commentators and modern archaeological scholars, the chief characteristics of the local populace were:

a) an aversion to and a lack of skill in intensive agriculture;

b) a marked disinclination to live in permanent villages.

So, unless they mugged it up on the boat coming over, these Anglo-Saxons were one of the most remarkable tribes ever to have come out of Germania. But this is where Applied Epistemology can lend a hand to explain why this anomaly persists. Whenever there's an insoluble anomaly, academia makes sure that there's a carefully inserted fissure just where the anomaly is. That way, neither side need take responsibility. (Actually, this isn't exactly *arranged*, it's more that since the fissure can't be closed, two discrete disciplines start to grow on either side, but the effect is the same.) It will be recalled that for all practical purposes the Anglo-Saxons don't exist in Germany or southern Scandinavia, so they aren't studied by German or Scandinavian scholars. Or, more precisely, if any German or Scandinavian scholar wishes to investigate the Anglo-Saxons, he or she has to come to Britain to learn what's what. So the entire history (there is no pre-history) of the Anglo-Saxons is a strictly British matter, subject to British paradigms. Now the British aren't in the least concerned about German tribes, or if they are they have to go and study them in German universities using German paradigms, so they're guaranteed not to learn anything about the German Anglo-Saxons. So the twain never meet. Both sides are, maybe, aware that there's an anomaly present, but neither side is in a position to do anything about it. So the anomaly just sits there until a passing Applied Epistemologist takes an interest, only to be met with a unanimous Anglo-German retort: 'What do you know about any of this? It takes years of study.' And in a sense they're right. You don't learn how to isolate anomalies in kindergarten.

In case you're wondering what really did happen to those thousands of missing villages, ask yourself where it is that modern archaeologists can never carry out village-sized investigations and the answer becomes obvious. But if you're still wondering, the solution is at the end of the next chapter.

Anomaly Five: How Many Loan-words Can One Language Bear?

All languages have 'loan-words', words borrowed from or adapted from foreign languages to describe things for which there's no local equivalent. Before the present technological era there was little requirement for borrowing words, because innovation was conducted at a leisurely pace and there wasn't much by way of trade in exotic goods. The only obvious exception was when people speaking a different language from the natives occupied a given country, in which case various terms, mainly of a military and administrative nature, would be introduced and very often permanently adopted into the native language. An even more pronounced version of this is when the foreigners have a written language and the locals do not, since becoming 'civilised' (a technical term, not a judgemental one) requires a comparative raft of new words. Nevertheless, it would be unusual in any circumstances for loan-words to rise to the hundreds out of a total of several tens of thousands of existing native words. English, as per usual, is a striking departure from this universal pattern.

English has tens of thousands of 'Latinate' words – i.e. cognate with Latin or French – the rest being 'Germanic' words, cognate with German, Danish, Old Norse, etc. ('Cognate' words are either the same as those in another language or corrupted or evolved versions of them.) There's quite a bit of etymological uncertainty (to say the least), but the normally quoted ratio is two-thirds Germanic to one-third Latinate. This in turn leads linguists to define English as being a 'Germanic language with considerable Latinate borrowings'. Anglo-Saxon has virtually no Latinate content and is defined as a purely Germanic language. This situation is of course unsurprising in the case of Anglo-Saxon, since the Anglo-Saxons lived outside the Roman Empire and didn't have much contact with any Latinate speakers. But the question then arises: 'How did Anglo-Saxon acquire an inordinate number of Latinate words as it metamorphosed into English?'

The most obvious source is from the Romano-British since, according to the official account, the Romano-British were mainly Welsh-speakers who

a) were civilised by and lived intimately with the Romans for several centuries, and

b) in turn civilised and lived intimately with the Anglo-Saxons for several centuries.

But the Romano-Brits can't be cited as a source, even by officialdom, because while the several hundred Latinate coinings in Welsh are indeed mostly concerned with 'civilised values' (*eglwys*=church, *ffenestr*=window, *cloch*=bell, *llyfr*=book, *sebon*= soap, etc.), none of these reached either Anglo-Saxon or English. This is a bit baffling if the official account is true. Perhaps the Anglo-Saxons didn't use soap.

It's often vaguely mooted that the Roman Catholic Church was the source for at least some of the Latinate content of English, but this can't be the case either, because then these Latinate words would be present in later Anglo-Saxon (i.e. once the Anglo-Saxons had converted to Roman Christianity), which they aren't (with the exception of a handful of strictly Church terms). Nor could Latinate words have been introduced via any of the other groups who invaded and occupied England from time to time – Danes, Norwegians, Picts, Irish – because none of these languages has any discernible Latinate content. Which leaves the Normans, and since they spoke the entirely Latinate language of French, the Normans have become the official source for pretty much the totality of the tens of thousands of Latinate words that had managed to worm their way into English by the time it re-emerged in written form in the late medieval period. There is, you will be unsurprised to hear, no actual evidence that the Normans did any such thing (apart from the usual regime-change coinages like *Parliament*, *royalty*, *motte-and-bailey* and so forth), but since the Latinate content of English 'must have come from the Normans', no evidence has ever been deemed necessary.

Actually, it's a shame that orthodoxy doesn't address the issue, because now we'll never get the answers to a number of tantalising questions:

1. The Normans didn't introduce writing, didn't introduce a new religion, in fact were virtually identical to the Anglo-Saxons in terms of general culture (perhaps even a shade behind), so why were the latter so anxious to adopt so many words from the former?

2. How exactly did the very few Normans manage to persuade the millions of natives to adopt tens of thousands of Latinate versions of words they already had? Did the Sheriff of Nottingham run language classes?

3. Why did the Normans leave almost no trace of their language wherever else they went – Ireland, Calabria, Sicily, Greece, and Normandy itself (where they arrived speaking Norse) – and yet managed to change a third of the entire English language in England?

4. The Normans ruled England with tight central control, so it would be at least technically possible to engineer a linguistic revolution. But how did they trigger the same linguistic revolution in lowland Scotland where, with the best will in the world, their rule amounted to little more than ineffectual kings and a rather feckless baronage?

* * *

So many anomalies, so many unanswerable questions. There must be a matrix on which this quite spectacular armada of errors sits. For people, expert or lay, to believe such nonsense with such fervent certainty there must be some underlying dogma that's leading them astray. They just can't all be that stupid. Let's find out what it is.

Chapter Two

Creating Myths

We can, I think, agree that there's a prima facie case that some kind of creation myth may be present in the current version of British history, but what exactly is it? Gimlet-eyed readers will have spotted no fewer than four creation myths embedded in the orthodox account, though, to be technical, there's one creation myth and three 'discontinuities':

The *fons et origo*: the Ice Age and the appearance of the First Men (the Stonehenge-builders);

First Discontinuity: the First Men depart, a new base population appears (the Celts);

Second Discontinuity: the 'heroes of the story' appear (the Anglo-Saxons);

Third Discontinuity: the current state is established (by the Normans).

This is always presented as straightforward history, but it's actually a straightforward steal from the Christian Creation Myth:

The *fons et origo*: the Creation and the appearance of Adam and Eve;

First Discontinuity: the Flood removes the First Men and Noah's Ark provides a new base population;

Second Discontinuity: the 'heroes of the story' appear (the Israelites);

Third Discontinuity: the 'current state' is established (by Jesus and the Christians).

But it's not entirely surprising that creation myths tend to follow general rules, because they always have to satisfy the same three conditions:

1. To be credible, i.e. not obviously at variance with the known facts.

2. To be complete, i.e. take the story from the beginning to the present without undue gaps.

3. To reflect credit on the people for whom and by whom they are composed.

This isn't easy because when little is known, continuity is a problem; and when a lot is known, it may not reflect credit. Fortunately, creation myth-makers have one or two tricks-of-the-trade to fall back on. The starting point, for example, is always some kind of blank canvas that both blots out everything that went before and offers up a pristine world upon which one's own story can unfold. This may sound technically difficult, but anything will serve so long as it's believable to your audience. (And remember, with creation myths the audience is only too anxious to believe *something*.) The Judaeo-Christians go for a 'Divine Creation', academic historians prefer an 'Ice Age', but they are both good of their genre.

The 'First Men' present more of a problem. While they can simply be 'wished into existence', since they 'must have existed', they are subject to a somewhat vexing characteristic: human fissiparity being what it is, one's own First Men are very likely to be a lot of other people's First Men as well, and so of limited utility for one's own creation myth. Best practice is to:

a) wish them into existence;

b) demonstrate some unique connection with your own story;

c) get rid.

Judaeo-Christians use the fairly bludgeonsome model often favoured by Ancient civilisations:

a) Omniscient Mystery Being creates First Men (God, Adam, Eve);

b) lineage is forged between First Men and one's own founding fathers (A begat B begat C, etc.);

c) flood sweeps everyone else away.

Obviously our own modern scholars can't use such relatively primitive methods because:

a) they have rather more in the way of 'known facts' that they have to allow for;

b) their audience has a more sceptical attitude towards Omniscient Mystery Beings;

   c) not to mention World-Wide Catastrophe Theory;

   d) they don't have control over their own starting point.

This last is the really critical factor. In traditional societies, the people responsible for religion are also the people responsible for creation myths, so naturally God provides both the story and the evidence for that story. Christians offer Biblical evidence as proof of the Biblical story: God creates Adam and Eve, God writes the Bible, the Bible says that God created Adam and Eve etc. This suffices for traditional believers (and modern morons), but today's historians have no such God-given powers; they have to fight it out with other academic disciplines in the race to provide the creation myth *de nos jours*. And while history is an important enough subject in its own sphere, it stands no chance against real academic colossi like the Space, Earth and Life Sciences. It's these 'sciences' (not that they're necessarily sciences) that nowadays get to write the creation myths, and historians have to spatchcock in their own requirements as best they can.

The situation, as modern historians found it, was roughly thus:

1. Copernicus/Kepler/Newton had established the potentially God-free universe.

2. Hutton and the early Earth Science pioneers had established that there were no particular time constraints. As far as they were concerned, the Earth was millions (later, billions) of years old and, unlike the previous paradigm, there was no need to associate the start of Man with the start of Earth.

3. Darwin and the early Life Science pioneers had established that Man in fact came late, though not nearly as late as Genesis claimed. But there was some doubt whether 'Man' could be said to have started at all.

4. Historians understood that they would have to work within these parameters, but they also knew that human beings are temperamentally, possibly intellectually, incapable of fitting themselves into such an inchoate universe. They want to know their place, exactly and with certainty, and are prepared to put up with a certain amount of finagling to get it.

So historians came up with a neat trick. They divided the human past into history and *pre*-history so that pre-history did all the interfacing with the scientific stuff. Then they handed pre-history over to other subjects, ones which operate by the methods of the Life and Earth Sciences and so can't be realistically criticised for lack of methodological rigour by their parent bodies. Once you have divided your study into two halves, one inside the subject and one technically outside it, you can stuff all the anomalies into the one you don't officially control, so any time somebody points out a particularly blatant anomaly, a historian can just shrug: 'I quite agree, it's quite scandalous, what *are* they playing at?'

But this ploy does leave one very vulnerable point, and that is the junction between pre-history and history. (Of course, all the other junctions between the subjects making up pre-history and the 'sciences' are pretty suspect too, but that's no longer of concern to historians, though of intense interest to Applied Epistemologists.) It's essential that historians retain control over this critical point. This hasn't proved difficult, because pre-history has been broken down into a plethora of weak Balkan statelets – archaeology, palaeo-anthropology, dendrochronology, linguistics and suchlike – none of which can afford to stand up to the local great power of History (except archaeology is increasingly becoming a Serbia ready for a showdown with the ramshackle history empire). History has ordained that pre-history gives way to history as soon as writing appears, because this is the point at which historians know it's safe for them to take over.

The place for the handover is also called *Civilisation*, because it's assumed that writing is coeval with half-a-hundred other things, which might be reasonable in itself but, since the real reason is that history is entirely dependent on the single methodology of examining and interpreting contemporary documentation and so can hardly put the takeover at any other point, this is something we'll have to take their word for. This is not to say that it's other than an excellent methodology. What people wrote at the time is far and away the best guide to that otherwise inaccessible place, the past; or, to put it the other way round, relying solely on what was written at the time is far and away the best antidote to that otherwise extravagantly imagined place, the past. All very honourable, all very efficient, history goes from strength to strength. But as usual, there's a price to pay for this headlong advance. Certain corners have to be cut, and in those corners lurk the anomalies that won't go away. And they too go from strength to strength and will result sooner or later in a major paradigm crack-up. (Or so Applied Epistemologists hope.) Let's remind ourselves where these dark places are, so we can keep a lookout for subsequent mischief:

1. **Before writing begins.** Although everybody pays lip service to pre-civilised societies as being marvels of trade and metalwork, nobody really means it. It's strictly anthropology. Of course, it's not true that Germans lived in trackless forests just because the Roman propaganda said they did, but historians (not pre-historians, because there *is* Roman propaganda) assume that essentially Germans lived in trackless forests. They have to mention the metalwork because the archaeologists are actually turning the stuff up, but it never occurs to historians that in order to defeat the Romans there has to be a sophisticated German state. No writing means no state.

2. **Whenever writing disappears for a bit.** It's amazing what can happen during a Dark Age. Entire populations will disappear, everyone will change their language, entire creation myths get spawned whenever a sudden gap in the written record gives historians licence to make things up.

3. **When the written record is being consciously messed with.** It never occurs to historians that the people making the records are just like us. We take it as read that every government is tampering with the record, we even know that monopolistic governments like dictatorships and theocracies actually specially compose a spurious record, but whenever historians have to rely on a very thin written record, they swallow it whole. Well, there wouldn't be any history otherwise, would there?

4. **When the writers of the record are not interested in what we are interested in.** There are millions of animals in Britain today, and unless there's an outbreak of foot-and-mouth they never get in the papers. It's a bit like that with millions of peasants in Roman, Anglo-Saxon and Norman Britain.

5. **Or just plain don't know.** There's a reason why Greeks and Romans called everyone else barbarians. It's because they all sounded alike, baa-ing like sheep. So it's unwise to rely on Greek or Roman testimony when it comes to who was speaking what.

The 'flexibility' that comes from dividing history off from pre-history is particularly useful in the construction of creation myths. First Men leave artefacts but not writing, which puts them inside pre-history but outside history proper. This ambiguous status means that when a particular set of *national* historians have to account for, let's say, a nationally important set of ruins, they can annex them for creation myth purposes or set them aside, as needs must. *The History of Stonehenge* is a much shorter book than *The History of the History of Stonehenge*, but the one thing historians are all agreed on is that the monument was built by people now long gone. That way, whatever theory is currently favoured – and they range from an expensive means of deciding when spring has arrived to measuring the size of the Solar System – Stonehenge itself is insulated from British pre-history generally. Obviously you can't have people running around in animal skins and woad one minute, building a stone super-computer the next minute, and then returning to skin and woad. It's rather like trying to reconstruct 19th-century history when you can't be sure whether Jules Verne is a novelist or the Ministry of Science's chief archivist. A degree of sophistication, though, is required; historians have to have an eye on the long haul. For instance, depending on prevailing political vicissitudes, the ruins of Zimbabwe were built by a) mysterious, probably white, visitors; b) Arab traders; or c) the present-day inhabitants. The currently-favoured version – 'the locals dunnit' – is actually fraught with danger, since it's likely to attract the withering retort: 'Well, they haven't done much since, have they?' British historians would never fall for that one.

In properly composed creation myths, it's always safer for First Men to come from somewhere else, much as riots are always caused by 'outside agitators'. Early historians tended to go for heroic and tragic forebears from faraway places (Trojans were always a big favourite), but our own much more careful scholars are content with merely faraway places, inclining to areas of the world sufficiently remote to be enigmatic but not so remote as to invite unkind queries as to why human beings always seem to come *from* places they otherwise would not dream of going *to*. This 'somewhere else' is further constrained by another historical paradigm: everything worthwhile always comes from the east. In the British case, this means Rift Valley Africa or Central Asia for human beings generally, Mesopotamia and Egypt to begin 'history', Greece and Rome to introduce 'civilised values', Italy and France to usher in the modern, post-Renaissance world. Even English religion is held to be a German invention, though Lutheranism clearly started in Wycliffian England, got transferred to Hussite Bohemia via English dynastic politics and then across the border to Luther whence, admittedly, it was re-imported *de novo* into England. Whether historians' belief in an eastern dawn for everything is an unconscious survival of a mystic Sun Cult or is in fact what happened in history need not concern us for the moment, because where British creation myths are concerned, there's an obvious problem: Britain is at the western end of the world's largest land mass, and if everything is arriving from the east, how can one's own First Men be made special when they are merely the off-shoots, indeed the end-of-the-line, of a lot of other nations' First Men?

Fortunately, by some incredible fluke the British Isles division of these First Men was responsible for building Newgrange (in Ireland) and Stonehenge (in England), both of which were in advance of anything else in contemporary Europe, so they were indeed special. But, I hear you splutter into your soup, you thought that wasn't possible? Exactly! They couldn't therefore have been Ancient Britons, but a bunch of highly mysterious people (possibly from the east) who came, built and then disappeared, hence fulfilling the criteria of First Men in creation myths. The fact that megaliths form a neat curve around the western European littoral from the Orkneys to Morocco means, apparently, that these mysterious eastern people swept all the way across the Eurasian land-mass to the very edge of their known world, spent enormous time and energy building these apparently useless objects in what were for them the most remote locations they could find, then fucked off.

The next step in the composition of the creation myth is to move the story on from the First Men to the Chosen People. The key problem here is how to get your own lot in and the aboriginal lot out without raising a lot of woolly-minded concerns about whose land it is. And the solution is a neat one: *never have the Chosen People directly replacing the First Men.* First Men are special, which makes dispossessing them a form of parricide – possibly blasphemy – so what's needed is a *cut-out,* a bunch of intermediate, not-at-all-special people whose only role in history is to stand between the First Men and the Chosen People, thus attracting all the obloquy for disposing of the Good Guys, and who can therefore be disposed of with a clear conscience by the next lot of Good Guys.

The Bible, as usual, is our guide in these matters: the Israelites, you will recall, established their claim to the Promised Land for all time by some complicated negotiations involving God, Abraham and Isaac, whereupon the whole lot of them got somewhat mysteriously shunted off to Egypt and then came back and ousted the Canaanites, who equally mysteriously were now in occupation of the Promised Land. Now who in God's name are these Canaanites? Who cares? A blast on the trumpets, they're gone and, presto, you have the legitimisation of the Israelite state. This is a trick that can be pulled any time you find yourself in some remote Babylonic exile and some inconvenient bunch of no-hopers are currently occupying the *Heimat.* Notice you need never quite get round to defining who is an Israelite, how long you can be away before you lose occupancy rights, where exactly the homeland boundaries are, or what is the status of the current interlopers (rhymes with no-hopers). Nor – and this is important for our own story – does it matter what language is being spoken. The Israelites did have a unique language, Hebrew, but as far as we know nobody ever spoke it as a mother-tongue. They may have used Hebrew for various liturgical, legal and literary functions, but when it came to talking to one another the Israel-ites seem always to have spoken the ordinary *langues-de-pays* – Canaanite, Egyptian, Phoenician, Babylonian, Aramaic, Greek, Arabic. Only in 1947 when they found themselves speaking literally outlandish languages – German, Yiddish, Polish, Russian, Hindi, English – were they obliged actually to start speaking Hebrew.

But back to the British. Superficially they seem to be in a far superior position on their island fastness right out there on the further reaches of Eurasia. Yet lo! they adopt the same model as people inhabiting the fast lane of the Fertile Crescent:

1. the disappearing First Men (the Stonehenge-builders);

2. the intermediate cut-outs (the Celts);

3. the Chosen People (the Anglo-Saxons).

This does, though, present a problem for British historians that their Biblical counterparts could afford to ignore amidst the maelstrom: to come up with a rational explanation for the singular fact that, in Britain, length of occupation is inversely proportional to present numbers:

1. the original inhabitants, the Stonehenge-builders, are now non-existent;

2. the Celtic-speakers who replaced them are presently a remnant population out on the western margins;

3. the folk who arrived just the other day, the English-speakers, comprise 99 per cent of the population.

Luckily, there's a handy historical model that permits just this situation: each wave of invaders ousts the last lot by whatever means it takes (murder, intermarriage, superior breeding rates, pushing them ever westwards, compulsory language lessons for the young – whatever is politically feasible at the time of writing); but unluckily, in the British case, this model simply doesn't work because the Anglo-Saxons *were not able to end the process*. Both the Danes and the Normans arrived on exactly the same basis as, but *after*, the Anglo-Saxons and yet failed miserably to produce a British population either 99 per cent Danish-speaking or 99 per cent French-speaking. However, British historians had the perfect answer to this one too. They ignored it.

It's often difficult for laypeople to comprehend how academics can be wilfully blind about fundamental aspects of their subject, but this is because of the way academic disciplines are structured. Subjects can be divided into two sorts:

a) **Those that are *vertically* organised**, i.e. everybody gets the same grounding, everybody moves on up the various branches, and only finally at the very highest level does true specialisation occur. Every mathematician, for example, irrespective of what arcane branch he ends up specialising in, is completely grounded in the basics of his subject. This reflects the fact that his arcane specialisation is itself grounded in the basics. Each layer is set on the firm foundations of what went before and, even more important, the basics truly are basic – Boolean Geometry depends on the angles of a triangle adding up to half the degrees in a circle.

b) **Those that are *horizontally* organised** – in other

words, irrespective of any token attempt at a generalist picture, it really comes down to: 'Welcome to your first history lesson. 1066 was an important year in ...' Maybe the students will do a bit of Anglo-Saxon stuff later on, maybe they won't, but the average history academic has no greater grasp of Dark Age Britain than the average history buff. Or worse, given that specialisation kicks in so very early, he will actually have less, leaving him with vague notions picked up in primary school and left festering ever since.

In *vertically* organised subjects, anomalies – unsolved problems generally – are much savoured. Everyone knows that the next big breakthrough is likely to come from their resolution. In *horizontally* organised subjects, unsolved problems have quite a different meaning – they may well be harbingers of a complete paradigm crack-up. To you and me, a paradigm crack-up would appear to be the most exciting thing imaginable in an academic career, but that's because we love intellectual excitement. To an academic it's pure poison, and that's because he has a mortgage to pay. Including, of course, an intellectual mortgage – an academic has invested his whole life in the learning and exposition of a certain set of facts and it's too much to ask that he retrain at his time of life.

All this leads to what Applied Epistemologists call 'careful ignoral', the chief method by which academics ensure that anomalies don't impinge on the general thrust of a subject. Here's a practical demonstration of how it works. Next time you find yourself in the History Department of a major university, trot up to some harmless academic type and say:

'Hey, you, Mr History Expert, just how did a few boatloads of rude Anglo-Saxon barbarians manage to completely replace several million Celtic-speakers who, after several centuries of Roman rule, were among the most culturally-advanced people on Earth?' In the slightly uncomfortable period before Security arrives, your scholarly interlocutor (who actually rather enjoys explaining technical matters to laypersons) will deal with your question by going through a standard list of academic avoidance procedures:

a) 'They just did', will be his first stab, safe in the knowledge that in the Dark Ages there's little historical evidence of anything one way or the other. Don't point out that there being no evidence of much happening may indicate that nothing much was happening, because the expert is not here being disingenuously dismissive, he's merely stating what for him is a known fact of history. It's not that he regards non-Anglo-Saxon origins as being beyond the bounds of rational debate; he regards the possibility of his profession getting such a basic thing wrong as being beyond the bounds of rational debate. It is, for him, literally unthinkable. Or, as he would put it: 'The evidence is overwhelming.' It certainly overwhelmed him.

b) On further reflection, i.e. in response to your scornful expostulations, our expert will appreciate that he's being asked, *qua* his status as an expert, to provide a specific reason for the Anglo-Saxon takeover. He will also instantaneously realise that he, personally, at this present moment in time, is not actually in possession of that reason. What he will therefore do is produce a reason that he knows, *vide* his being an expert, will 'fit the bill' – something that almost certainly must have happened (since it did happen), but expressed in technical language. In this case it's likely to be a fairly maundering tale of superior breeding rates in emigrant populations, or perhaps the propensity for ethnic cleansing among Dark Age warrior elites, or it could be the effect of the introduction of writing on advancing language clines, or then again it … well, the list is inexhaustible since it's being made up on the spot but, be assured, any reason advanced will be perfectly rational and completely plausible. It's important again to bear in mind that the expert isn't putting these things forward in any cynical or dishonest way – he truly believes what he's saying, even though he has almost certainly never thought about it in his entire professional life. His interior reasoning goes something like this:

i)   this is obviously a fundamental question for which a satisfactory explanation must have been reached by my colleagues at some time in the past (or at any rate has been the subject of inconclusive debate among them);

ii) as a fundamental matter, the correct explanation (or possible explanations) was probably taught to me in my undergraduate days and, presumably, either I wasn't paying attention or else I have forgotten it in the meantime;

iii) however, even the best undergraduate education can be patchy (for administrative reasons I now understand only too well) and I may not have acquired the knowledge formally at all but, since this is a fundamental matter, I would expect to have acquired it in general outline (or by extrapolation from similar processes elsewhere) in the ordinary course of intellectual osmosis at some time during my professional career;

iv) and since a perfectly reasonable explanation did pop into my head when I did think about it, it must indeed have been there all the time.

c) If you question this explanation, and you would yourself have to be a bit of an expert to do so, the expert will modestly agree with the shortcomings of his own explanation and *pass the professional buck*. History, being a horizontally organised subject which is not internally grounded, must always have the option of appealing to an outside authority to buttress its own shaky foundations. In this case, the question of Anglo-Saxon origins might go along these lines:

i) **Historian:** 'Yes, this is a historical question, but not one that falls within my remit. You'll have to talk to an Early Medievalist.'

ii) **Early Medievalist:** 'Yes, this is a question that technically falls within my remit, but it's not primarily a historical question. You're asking for a judgement on a linguistic matter, and should therefore consult a linguist.'

iii) **Linguist:** 'Yes, this is a question that technically falls within my remit, but it's one of such importance that a sub-category of specialists has come into existence to study it – the Anglo-Saxon and Middle English experts, whom you will find in the English Department.'

iv) **Middle English Specialist:** 'Yes, this is a question that technically falls within my remit, but this is not, as we would understand it, a problem of literature. In so far as it pertains to language morphology, it's a problem for linguists; in so far as the evidence is wholly derived from a small number of historical documents, it's a historiographical problem. Either/or, but I'm sure they'll sort it out for you.'

Again, it must be borne in mind that nobody here is being other than scrupulously professional. Being a specialist means knowing when to concede to another specialist, and it's not the fault of any individual that he works within a system that has specialisation as its operating principle. But supposing we, the people picking up the tab for all these specialists, rise up and demand that a Blue Riband Panel be set up to solve the Anglo-Saxon problem once and for all, what would happen? Something very interesting, something very revealing of the structural weaknesses of academia, something that stymies Applied Epistemologists at every turn. Anglo-Saxon specialists drawn from various disciplines would be gathered together and they would find themselves faced with a perplexing dilemma: the only reason why there are Anglo-Saxon specialists in the first place – as opposed to, say, Anglo-Danish specialists or Britanno-Norman-French specialists – is because Anglo-Saxon is deemed to be the forerunner of the English language and the Anglo-Saxons to be the forebears of the English people, and therefore inherently worthy of specialist study. If this be not so, then the whole justification for their existence is gone. Of course there will still be need of scholars to study an interesting period in British history, and there will still be need of people to study that very fascinating language, Anglo-Saxon, but the idea that a separate discipline is needed or that hapless generations of Eng. Lit. students should be required to study it becomes risible. So, on the narrow technical question of whether Anglo-Saxon did or did not evolve into English, will the turkeys vote for Christmas or will they reluctantly come to the conclusion that further research is needed?

In theory, we ought to look to archaeologists for assistance in this general area because we're dealing with the abutment between history and pre-history but, as we have seen, archaeology is a daughter-discipline of history and is obliged to accept historical paradigms when formulating its own theories. The fact that 'history rests literally on archaeology but Archaeology rests on History' leads, as one might imagine, to some gloriously Alice-in-Wonderland situations whenever historians provide archaeologists with duff assumptions. When archaeologists are forced to reconcile what they're finding in the ground with what historians tell them they ought to be finding in the ground, it's the archaeologists that have to do the explaining away. It tells us a lot about archaeologists that they always manage it somehow.

This is a problem that plagues the whole of early history. The most absurd, because most important, is the case of the 'missing half-millennium'. Historians use Egyptian king-lists to establish a basic chronology for Egypt during the first two millennia BC and, because all the contemporary Middle and Near East states corresponded with the Egyptians, everybody's archival record can be neatly dovetailed together, giving us a nice coherent chronology for Ancient History as a whole. However, as luck would have it, the Egyptian king-lists have turned out to be hopelessly corrupt, and several centuries of completely spurious time have been inserted (by modern historians) into the true Pharaonic history. This in turn puts everybody else's chronology out. In a rational world this would quickly be spotted by either historians or archaeologists reporting that so many anomalies were turning up in so many different places, something must be wrong with the basic chronology, and a better one would be worked out. But three wholly characteristic circumstances have thus far prevented this from happening:

1. Egyptology is far and away the senior branch of Ancient History, so what it says goes as far as other historians are concerned;

2. historians don't take kindly to being corrected by archaeologists (muck-shifters, the lot of them);

3. the Near East during the first two millennia BC is prime creation myth territory for a variety of national, cultural

and religious interests, and it rather suits everybody that nobody can quite make head or tail of the fact that, for instance, the Bible (which is pretty good history) never seems to tally up with Egyptian history.

So everyone has been told to pipe down and explain away the anomalies as best they can. Odd as it may seem, everybody is perfectly happy to do this because they have been brought up on historical paradigms, and human beings much prefer to be part of a broad church than to be heretics in the wilderness. Since all practitioners 'know' that historical assumptions are true, every time they find something that contradicts a historical assumption it can only mean that there must be something wrong with their own work.

One would think this to be disagreeable, but that is to misunderstand the nature of academic paradigms. Individual practitioners thrive on contradictions. Any competent observer can write up a description of a hole full of grave goods; it takes an expert to explain why they appear to be in the wrong order. It takes a very adept archaeologist to make 'It must 'ave slipped down from a higher strata, squire' into a formula acceptable to a learned journal. Of course, individual archaeologists might from time to time wonder why their work is constantly having to be explained away, they might even on occasion try to argue the toss, but thanks to the democratic centralism of peer-review, only the proper conclusion ever gets written up. And since just being an archaeologist requires publishing peer-reviewed papers, it's better to thrive on contradictions than point them out.

Looking at things from outside the cosy world of history-

and-archaeology, all this can be pretty funny. Rum things crawl out from the historical record when several hundred years of spurious time have somehow got themselves inserted into the real world: either the same event occurs twice at either end of the non-existent several hundred years, or on-going processes get put on hold for several hundred years while the real world waits for the historical record to catch up. Hence textbooks end up saying, with a perfectly straight face, things like:

a) The Ancient Greeks fight the Trojan War, operate the Mycenean and Minoan civilisations and generally dominate the eastern end of the Mediterranean in the 13th century BC, then they disappear from history for 500 years, then they turn up again in the 8th century BC doing all the things they were doing 500 years before, as though they'd never been away. (Historians' verdict: 'We have termed this 500-year period when nothing seems to be happening "The Greek Dark Ages".')

b) An Egyptian pharaoh builds a canal linking the Nile with the Red Sea and opens it with a tremendous fan-fare. Five hundred years later, Pharaoh builds the same canal in the same place and opens it again with a tremendous fanfare. (Historians' verdict: 'He must have been deepening and widening the existing canal but not wishing to give credit to a Pharaoh of a previous dynasty.')

c) Six Hittite kings turn up bearing the same names, in the same sequence, as six Hittite kings of 500 years before. (Historians' verdict: 'An extraordinary tribute to dynastic forebears.')

British archaeologists naturally suffer their own local difficulties whenever they're obliged to obey false *British* historical paradigms. They too have to construct wondrously circular arguments to tie up the loose ends resulting from British historians ordering them to come to a point that never existed in history. Thus, almost all English villages have English names, and since place-names tend not to change much, this means that the villages of England must have been largely founded by English-speakers. If 'English-speakers' didn't pitch up until the 6th, 7th, 8th centuries AD, in the guise of Anglo-Saxons, this means that English villages are no older than 1,500 years. So far so good; it's an entirely internal argument. However, some of these 'Anglo-Saxon' villages are surrounded by 'hedgebanks' – very ancient embankments made of earth, stone, vegetation, etc. – which are slightly mysterious in function but may have been boundaries, or protection from man or beast, or created by passing traffic in sunken lanes, or for ritualistic purposes or … well, it doesn't really matter, because it's the *age* of the hedgebanks that's at issue. Clearly they can't be older than their associated villages, and the associated villages are known to be no older than 1,500 years. But hedgebanks *can* be dated. Uh-oh. Dating hedgebanks doesn't come under history's aegis; it's a strictly botanical matter, and Botany doesn't kowtow to anyone in the academic firmament. So what happens if the two sides come up with wildly conflicting dates? Let's watch as the merry pranksters dance round this one.

Plants establish themselves in hedges (and hedgebanks) at a constant rate over time – that rate being approximately one woody species per hundred years in every hundred feet of hedge (Hooper's Law) – so by counting the species that have established themselves, the age of any hedge can be roughly calculated. This is all a bit new, all a bit conjectural, and it hasn't entirely made it as a scientific doctrine, but hopes are high that it will eventually take its place as one of the Life Sciences' manifold contributions to the advancement of human knowledge. However, the botanists aren't entirely judge-and-jury because

1. to check the efficacy of the method you need to know the actual age of a fair sample of hedges, and only historians – using maps, documents, etc. – can provide that data;

2. there's no botanical reason to know the age of a hedge (except occasionally a very old hedge is useful ammunition in gaining recognition for a Site of Special Scientific Interest);

3. there's only one useful purpose for dating hedges, and that's to provide historians with data where there are no maps, documents, etc. to show the age of hedges.

So gradually, what started out as pure botany becomes a kind of joint enterprise, in fact a branch of archaeobotany, which in practice is yet another minor adjunct of the history empire. Botany itself soon takes little further interest, being merely satisfied that one of its little buds has proved useful and gets the parent body some much needed exposure via all those archaeological telly programmes.

The historians, though, are mightily pleased; they have a bit of underpinning from a genuine science. Meanwhile, what of the age of the hedgebanks themselves? Well, there everybody has run into a bit of a snag. Although it's true, in a theoretical sort of way, that species will establish themselves at a known rate, this is always subject to an upper limit – there are only so many hedge-loving plants in any given ecology. That number in lowland Britain is about fifteen, so there can never be more than fifteen or so species in any hedge, no matter how old it is. So every time historians try to date an Anglo-Saxon hedgebank, they come up with the number fifteen – which, according to Hooper's Law, means the hedgebank is 1,500 years old. By Jove, it's Anglo-Saxon!

Perhaps you're wondering what would have happened if archaeobotany had produced a very ancient date for English village hedgebanks? Not much. We know this because similar situations are becoming more and more common in academia as the hard sciences are having more and more to justify their existence now that the Great Age Of Science For Its Own Sake is over. For instance, Genetics is all very lah-di-dah but what we really want from it is establishing paternity of children, catching criminals and treating medical disorders. For which Genetics is, of course, more than happy to offer up its DNA expertise. The same expertise allows it to offer its assistance with the vexed question of where the British population came from. But now they run slap bang into an equally vexed problem – the wretched historians have got this all wrong – which leaves the geneticists with a bit of a choice to make; they can either

1. tell it like it is and have the established experts (the historians) assure them that they've got it all wrong, that this new-fangled study of population genetics is completely out to lunch and they need to go away and get its methodology right; or

2. tell it like it isn't and curl up in a ball of guilt.

So naturally they don't adopt either course. Instead they produce a long string of studies packed full of impressive number-crunching but with curiously tentative conclusions hedged around with every kind of caveat. This then leaves historians to pick and choose the bits that support the paradigm ('Told you so, and now we can prove it.') and reject the bits that don't ('More research needed on this one, lads.'). This is fair enough in the rough-and-tumble world of pre-history, but the errors become structural when geneticists, setting out to establish their base-line assumptions, ask historians to provide them with some absolutely known samples. If you extract DNA from a pre-Roman English cemetery that you are assured is Celtic, you have a base-line for Celtic DNA. If you then measure the DNA of people living in central Ireland on the basis that they are likely to be Celtic in origin and you find that the two match, you've got a doubly-sure Celtic base-line. And they *will* match because, according to Applied Epistemologists, they are both representative of the English-speaking aboriginal British population. And just consider the confusion when you're measuring Anglo-Saxon DNA in the native British population when you don't know that in fact the native British population was speaking a language quite closely related to Anglo-Saxon and therefore already has a pre-existing DNA overlap. Round and round and round it goes, where it'll end nobody knows. Probably because if it did, everyone would be hurled off in a fearful tangle of limbs.

It might be noted here that one of the reasons why incorrect academic theories have such longevity is because of circularities unobtrusively finding their way into the chain of reasoning. Since the 'climax figure' – i.e. the maximum number of species that attach themselves to hedgebanks in English conditions – is the same as 'the computed Anglo-Saxon age', it follows that each time a hedgebank is measured, the present paradigm is reinforced. Fortunately, in 500 years or so the scales will finally drop, because by 2500 AD, Hooper's Law will be pointing to English villages being Norman creations, and even Norman specialists will have difficulty wearing that one. But generally these circularities don't get time-expired. Take the matter of the place-names of these villages. Any reputable guidebook will tell you that most English villages have names that derive from Anglo-Saxon terminology, which of course they must do if they were in fact founded by the Anglo-Saxons. What reputable guidebooks, and for that matter reputable historical, archaeological and linguistic textbooks omit to tell you is that by some malign historical mischance *we don't have a single example of a known Anglo-Saxon village-name*. This gap in the evidence arises from the fact that the Anglo-Saxons happen to be a tribe whose original homeland isn't precisely known, so we can't just pop over there and check out how they name their villages. We have only Anglo-Saxon villages in England to compare with Anglo-Saxon villages in England.

Problem? No, opportunity. Here's the standard operating procedure:

a) Record place-names in Germany, Frisia and Denmark (roughly where the Anglo-Saxons came from) and see if there are any affinities between these place-names and English place-names. Since virtually every single German, Frisian and Danish word has some sort of affinity with the corresponding English and/or Anglo-Saxon word, by virtue of them all being members of the same language group, a number of said affinities have been found.

b) List place-names suggested by a) in the one area known for certain to have been lived in by Anglo-Saxons (i.e. England) and declare the result to be a list of Anglo-Saxon place names.

So when you read in your guidebook that, say, Haggarstun is the *tun* (Anglo-Saxon for 'settlement') of the local Anglo-Saxon landowner, *Haggar*, you should bear in mind that

1. we have no way of knowing whether Haggar is an Anglo-Saxon name (we have almost no examples of contemporary English given names for comparative purposes);

2. we don't know that *tun* is an Anglo-Saxon word (the word means 'farmyard' in Danish and 'garden' in Dutch, but since all Anglo-Saxon words of which we have knowledge come from England, it may be a loan-word from a British language);

3. we do know that a thousand years later the word *tun* still exists in English and still means exactly the same thing (precisely so in dialect, viz. 'Toon Army', and, via a slight shift, in the Standard English 'town').

Now that you're something of an expert on English place-names, try your hand at some circular exegesis of your own. Why not start with my local 'Anglo-Saxon' settlement, Hammersmith. This, according to the place-name guidebook, is derived from the Anglo-Saxon *hammersmiththe*, meaning ... er ... hammer-smithy. Be pithy with your answer.

* * *

What are the wider lessons of all this? The most significant aspect of the foregoing is not whether it makes a convincing case but whether it makes a prima facie case. The human brain is quite good at teasing out correct solutions when put to the test, but it's much better at avoiding being put to the test in the first place. That's why in this book such emphasis is placed on scholars' failure to address anomalies. While my own explanations may or may not be acceptable, it's difficult to deny that various apparently significant problems are being routinely ignored by those on whom we look to rely.

English-speakers take it for granted that they speak a language derived from Anglo-Saxon (should they be disposed to think about it at all), but the question arises as to why, or perhaps how, they can arrive with such confidence at such an answer. It's because they don't *arrive* at it at all. They *start* from it. It's a melancholy but irresistible fact that every single British historian, long before he or she ever knows he or she is to be a historian, is under the fixed impression that English is derived from Anglo-Saxon, and that this is a self-evident truth attested to by every single British historian, which means that they're unlikely even to listen to alternatives. But just to make it doubly difficult, one cannot demolish modern creation myths by direct methods of refutation because creation myths – and academic paradigm theories in general – are almost invariably, in the jargon, 'not falsifiable'. In essence they always contain some combination of circular argument and untestable assumption that renders them unassailable to normal evidential methods. This doesn't make them valueless, or even necessarily untrue, but it does give them infinite life, whether true or false.

Perhaps this is understandable enough in an area like British pre-history with all its enigmatic silences, but the general problem goes far wider. Take the exemplar of all modern academic paradigms, the Theory of Evolution. There's no question that the theory is valuable in so far as it has led more or less directly to the creation of the modern Life Sciences, but, true or false, the theory no less certainly contains the seeds of its own infinite survival. Having adopted a properly scientific root-and-branch model of speciation in which *ex hypothesi* all species must be demonstrably linked to other species, it permits the indefinite opening of new categories whenever a species *cannot* be demonstrably linked to other species. This has the unavoidable corollary that nothing can ever be discovered from now until the end of time that can ever call the model into question. This isn't quite the same as saying, as an academic biologist would, 'The reason why we shall never find a species that contradicts Darwinian

Evolution is because all species arose by Darwinian Evolution.' Though of course this may also be true.

This indefinite 'opening of new categories' is, according to Occam's Razor, supposed to be the signal of a failing paradigm; but the difficulty is that there's no mechanism to call a halt, to say 'enough is enough, the model is too complex to be the right model'. If a theory is so powerful as to have built the modern Life Sciences, nobody is going to say that the emperor is wearing far too many clothes. Only when a new and better theory comes along does anyone notice how absurdly encrusted was the old system. Nor is it true that the Academy likes simplicity, elegance, models with the fewest working parts: the discovery of yet another ill-fitting species fills the Life Scientists not with gloom because their cherished system has been called into question by having yet another epicycle tacked on to an existing epicycle; no, there's universal rejoicing that now they have a brand new box of tricks for everyone to play with, a brand new speciality with its own brand new specialists. The Life Sciences just got bigger.

In the humanities, of course, there's a widespread resistance to the very idea of modelling human behaviour. 'Let the facts speak for themselves' is the watchword, but this generally means that models creep in without being declared as such – usually in the guise of 'conventionally accepted descriptive systems'. These cannot be challenged without running into the unanswerable defence: 'Oh, that's just our conventional descriptive system, it's simply a matter of convenience, something we've all got used to over the years, we know quite well that the various categories are simply shorthand, with only a limited validity in themselves' – thus remaining embedded at the heart of their subject, unremarked, unexamined, untrue. An added bonus (or perhaps it's the point) is that the jargon of 'conventional descriptive systems' quickly becomes an argot, an infallible guide for recognising fellow-initiates. You have to have a university degree to be an –ologist and you have to be an –ologist to be able to speak to another –ologist about –ology. In such a closed shop, it's not so much that anomalies grow unchecked free from the fear of Occam's Razor; it's that the anomalies actually start to form such ornate epicycles on the once smooth certainties of the 'conventional descriptive systems' that entire sub-disciplines grow up to study them, until eventually the whole field is so unfathomably complex that you really do have to be an –ologist to understand the –ology. And by then it's far too late.

This syndrome has an added twist in the case of history. History is a story, no doubt a true story, but a story all the same with a beginning, a middle and an end, with heroes and villains, plot-lines, conflicts, denouements, good times and bad. When there's plenty of material, as in the modern age, it's a matter of judicious selection; in earlier years, it's a question of fitting scattered bits together. In pre-history, there's scarcely enough for a narrative at all, so what hope then that a revisionist theory that urges simplification will flourish? 'Come and study Ancient Britain; not much happened.'

But help is at hand. Occam's Razor still exists. When the basic paradigm is wrong, the professional practitioners are constantly, if blithely, turning up data in their day-to-day work that actually worsens the anomalies. And since the data itself is scrupulously correct, it eventually becomes a straight-forward proposition for the professional revisionist to draw all the anomalies together for the final cull. In the case of Early British History, the anomalies have been building up for so long and are arrayed in such neatly ordered ranks that the scythe really ought to take all the poppy-heads off with one grand swish. The anomalies will presumptively disappear once the creation myth is removed, and since creation myths are all about people arriving in a given place from somewhere else, the obvious step is to proceed on the assumption that the present British population has always lived more or less where it's living now, and see if the result makes better historical sense than the orthodox version. Applying this not-very-radical assumption to Britain would produce a history something like this:

Time immemorial
English-speakers occupy the British Isles.

Some time later
Celtic-speakers arrive by sea from the west and as 'sea-people' are able to replace the English-speakers anywhere immediately adjacent to the western seas, i.e. western Ireland, highlands and islands of Scotland, Cumbria, west Wales, Cornwall.

Up to 13th century AD
Various invaders come and go, setting up ruling regimes over the locals, whether English- or Celtic-speaking.

13th century onwards
When the invasions stop, the ruling regimes gradually become synonymous with the general population. The most populous of these (the English-speakers) become dominant

95

in England and Scotland. The minority Celtic-speakers gradually give way in all parts of the British Isles.

Not very exciting, but does it remove the anomalies we looked at in Chapter One?

Anomaly One

The Anglo-Saxons are now no longer the only barbarians in European history who managed to change an entire country's language. They arrived speaking Anglo-Saxon, they ruled over a population of English-speakers (and a few Celtic-speakers in Cornwall and Cumbria) and they were still speaking Anglo-Saxon when they were ousted as a ruling elite by the Danes partially and then the Normans wholly. The endless academic debate about whether the Anglo-Saxons got rid of the existing Celtic-speaking population in England by either wholesale acts of ethnic cleansing (the 'exterminationist' school) or by the less gruesome methods of intermarriage and peer persuasion (the 'integrationist' school) can now finally be resolved. They were both wrong.

Anomaly Two

The *Anglo-Saxon Chronicle* distinguishes between the 'British' and the 'Welsh' because with the breakdown of the Roman Empire there was an unavoidable return to a more primitive 'tribal' unit. Clearly there could be no return to the states described by Caesar after several centuries of Roman rule, so the only alternative would presumably be groupings based on language affinity. The two largest of these, on the revisionist reading, are English and Welsh, but since the Anglo-Saxons reserved the term 'English' for themselves, these would be referred to by them as *British* and Welsh. This 'British' that the *Anglo-Saxon Chronicle* refers to now ceases to be a highly unusual example of a modern European language expunged from the annals of linguistic history and turns out to be what we nowadays call 'English'.

The Cornish anomaly disappears too, because the Anglo-Saxons were no more interested in extirpating them than they were their English-speaking subjects in the rest of Britain, though it's true that over the next thousand years the Cornish, like all the other Celtic minorities in every corner of Western Europe, gradually succumbed to the linguistic dominance of the 'metropolitan' language (in their case, English). We know from place-name evidence that the original Celtic-speaking area in south-west England was much smaller than the equivalent areas in Wales, Scotland and Ireland, which is why their final demise was as 'early' as the 18th century. It remains to be seen when (or whether) the same phenomenon occurs in Wales, Scotland and Ireland.

A persistent loose end in Scottish history is also cleared up. The Picts are consistently portrayed as being a tribe of extremely violent, aggressive, red-headed people living in (though often sallying out of) the highlands of Scotland, a description uncannily close to later English and lowland Scots' views of the Gaelic highlanders. Many people have made the obvious connection that the one is in fact the other, but this has always run into the orthodox objection that in Pictish times it was the inhabitants of England and lowland Scotland that were assumed to be the Celtic-speakers, so the

Picts have been obliged to be some other language group entirely that somehow got lost in the Scotch mist. If the inhabitants of lowland Scotland were then exactly who they are now, the Picts can finally be the people they always were, the Scots Gaels of the highlands and islands.

Anomaly Three

Anglo-Saxon did not change its entire vocabulary in the couple of hundred years between the 12th and 14th centuries – it remained exactly what it had been since the 6th century and died out in a perfectly natural way once its speakers, the Anglo-Saxon ruling caste, were overthrown in 1066, in the same way that Belgic, Latin, Danish and Norman-French ceased to be spoken in Britain when those ruling castes were no longer ruling castes. Nor, looking at things from the other end of the telescope, did English change radically during that time, or indeed at any time. The English of Gladstone was a fair approximation of the English of Shakespeare which was a fair approximation of the English of Chaucer which was a fair approximation of the English being spoken when Julius Caesar arrived.

Anomaly Four

The reason why there's a lack of archaeological evidence of pre-Roman settlement is that the evidence is currently being lived in. In other words, the present villages and country towns of Britain *are* the archaeological evidence of pre-Roman settlement. The Iron Age Britons, the Romano-British, the post-Roman native population were all living in Winterbourne Abbas, Combe Lacey, Hartley Wintney, Kensington and

Chelsea and all the other places attested to as soon as English villages and towns were first set down in their totality, in the Domesday Book. It's one of the practical limitations of archaeology that it seldom digs in places where people live now; though whenever it does, it's remarkable how often sites turn out to be bottomless pits with no datable foundations other than the various face-saving epithets 'possibly Bronze Age', 'archaic', 'pre-Roman', 'of uncertain antiquity' and the rest. Contrariwise, the reason why so many 'high-status' sites are turned up by archaeologists is that before c. 1300 AD Britain was ruled by one foreign military caste after another (Celts, Belgae, Romans, Anglo-Saxons, Danes, Normans), and military castes always build 'high-status' communal buildings (variously called hill forts, long-houses, camps, villas, wassail-halls, manor houses, castles, cantonments, barracks, etc.) outside existing native villages and towns. And of course the Anglo-Saxons cease to be the only Germanic tribe with sophisticated agricultural and village-building pretensions; they found both on their arrival in Britain.

Although this is radical history, it's not at all radical anthropology. Anthropologists are quite aware that the *normal* pattern for all pre-modern intensive agricultural systems is the medieval one of common fields and villages. Even so, applying this picture to pre-historic Britain will run into violent opposition from pre-historians of every stripe, and especially archaeologists, who will claim that the evidence just doesn't bear it out. Ignoring the fact that archaeologists can jump through any number of hoops in the pursuit of a particular paradigm, there are two ways in which they can be helped towards seeing the blindingly obvious:

Abandoned villages

Here is the one case in which archaeologists can and do go in for whole-village digs, and they don't typically report very ancient origins (though they do typically report *some* Roman and pre-Roman finds). These villages are invariably described as being abandoned for one of two reasons:

a) some money-grabbing landlord has converted the area from arable to pastoralism, and hence the villagers have all had to go;

b) everybody died of the plague, so the village was abandoned.

Now neither of these reasons holds up at all. *Every* village in England could, if it were profitable, be converted from arable to pastoralism. It's just that it's extremely uncommon for areas that can sustain arable farming to be profitable for pastoralism. The only exception is when plague strikes and the price of agricultural labour goes up steeply. Then it's worthwhile converting the most marginal arable land to pastoral. But by the same token, the most marginal arable land is the last to be converted to arable land, so these villages tend to be very late. Hence 'abandoned villages' tend overwhelmingly to be 'late villages'. Another boring story of everyday country folk. But oh, how we do love our tales of grasping landlords and megadeath.

Wooden houses

Archaeology lives by its post-holes. And wooden structures always have post-holes. So Ancient Britain is a land of wooden housing, and where there are no post-holes, there are no houses, and no villages. Unfortunately this is complete tosh. The Ancient Brits lived in stone houses. How do we know this? Well, we don't. It's an application of '*What is* is *what was* unless it wasn't', and we all live in stone (or brick or concrete or anything except wood) houses now, so our ancestors likely did too, unless there's evidence that they didn't – and since there's a remarkable lack of the millions of post-holes that the millions of our ancient forebears would have required, that's pretty good negative evidence in its own right. But of course we can't rely on negative evidence, no matter how compelling, so we must fall back on common sense. Let me put it to you squarely: you're living in lowland Britain, where the forests have either all been felled or are jealously guarded for their enormously valuable timber. On the other hand, stone is everywhere and practically free. Dry-stone wall technology is everywhere too, and dry-stone wall technology is no different from house-wall technology. Oh, and by the way, stone lasts for ever but timber walling needs constant attention. And just one more factor: stone can't be dated and it doesn't leave post-holes, so you will be mystifying generations of archaeologists to come. Go on, which one will you choose?

Anomaly Five

The mystery of why English has so many Latinate words can be solved only after the creation myth of the French has been demolished in the next chapter. That's the best thing about revisionism – the more disciplined an academic discipline is, the easier the dominoes fall.

CHAPTER THREE

Tales of Romance

Whenever anyone is assured that English does not in fact derive from Anglo-Saxon, they always reply: 'So how come *English* is called *English* then? Doesn't English mean Angle?' This argument is advanced even by people who really ought to know better. People, for instance, who are well aware that *French* is not derived from *Frankish*. The situation in both countries is as follows:

1. Both England and France were originally called something else (Britain and Gaul respectively).

2. When the Romans left, both countries were invaded, occupied and ruled for several centuries by a Germanic people (the Anglo-Saxons and the Franks respectively).

3. These invaders gave their name to their new country (England and France respectively).

4. The inhabitants of these countries, invaders and natives alike, took their name from the country they lived in (the English and the French respectively).

5. When the invaders were long gone, the natives, for lack of any alternative, continued to call themselves English and French respectively.

6. So, rather naturally, they called the language they spoke after themselves (*English* and *French* respectively).

A bit later on, in fact many centuries on, the savants of both England and France felt impelled to investigate the origins of their respective languages and, as we know, linguists always hunt around for some convenient dead language that might fit the bill; and as soon as they've found one, they teach it as fact to their respective audiences until everyone is thoroughly convinced that it's self-evidently true. The English fastened on *Anglo-Saxon* but the French did not likewise fasten on *Frankish*, for two reasons:

1. *Frankish* as a Germanic language doesn't have the close family resemblance to *French* that *Anglo-Saxon* has to *English*, so it was impossible for them to make such a crass error.

2. *French* does have a close family resemblance to a much more prestigious dead language than either *Anglo-Saxon* or *Frankish*. So they fastened, with parallel crassness, on *Latin*.

As we all remember from our *Asterix* comics, the French were originally called Gauls and were a Celtic race. Again, just like the British, so perhaps it's time we came to grips with these ubiquitous yet oddly transient people, the Celts. They were well known to Classical writers (Celtae in Latin, Keltoi in

Greek), mostly because at periodic intervals they used to invade the Classical world, sack it, enslave it, put it to the sword and generally do all those things that Classical writers find worth writing about (in contrast to the ordinary people who rarely get a mention). These 'Celts' were described as being tall, blond, violently expansionist and inhabiting an area to the north of Italy and Greece. However, over the course of history one or two things must have changed, because the Celts as we know them today are small and dark, with a marked propensity for staying at home, which is at the westernmost extremities of Britain, Ireland, France and Spain. No explanation for this Celtic transformation has ever been vouchsafed.

Indeed, modern historians and linguists have made the problem worse by electing to assume that these Celts originally covered the British Isles, the Iberian peninsula, France, northern Italy, parts of the Balkans and even northern Turkey. So how exactly did the apparently largest language group in the whole of pre-historic Europe become practically the smallest one in modern Europe? Well, certainly there's no actual evidence that this ever happened. The orthodox explanation is 'It just did', which isn't very helpful. In fact, as usual, it's the fact that orthodoxy doesn't even address this epochal change that is the greatest mystery of all. Can we turn to the Celts themselves (that is, the Welsh, the Irish, the Scots Gaels and the Bretons) for assistance? Not really, because this is of course Celtic Creation Myth territory, and if your race was offered the choice between being

a) the most numerous people in the whole of pre-historic Europe, occupying a vast swathe of territory from the

Black Sea to the Atlantic and frequently acting as the military arbiters of the civilised world; or

b) a collection of tribes of the utmost obscurity existing with some difficulty at the furthermost margins of the known world ...

The Welsh, Irish, Scots Gaels and Bretons have gone for the first one.

So let's change the question slightly. How did the absurd notion that the largest language group in Europe could become the smallest one ever take hold in the imagination of academics? Now this *is* easy to answer. It all started in the 18th century when the Enlightenment reached Wales, and the Welsh-speaking intelligentsia felt it incumbent upon themselves to place *Welsh* in the great scheme of things. They knew that *Welsh* was very similar to *Cornish* and *Breton* and that it also had a close family resemblance to *Irish* and *Scots Gaelic*, but all these languages were very unlike *English*, *French* and *German*. As with all creation myths, there is a need to both plug yourself in but then make yourself special, so these Welsh savants

1. concluded (quite rightly) that *Welsh*, *Cornish*, *Breton*, *Gaelic* formed a language family;

2. then (rather dubiously) plugged themselves into *French*, *English* and *German* by the old ruse of opening a new category and arbitrarily joining their own branch alongside 'Germanic' and 'Romance' as another branch of the Western European language trunk;

3. then (quite meretriciously) cast around for a name for

their language branch and, since it wasn't being used by anyone else, purloined the name 'Celtic'.

Now, the usual thing happened. Since only *Welsh*-speakers have any knowledge of (or much interest in) *Welsh*, all the academics in this area were soon *Welsh*-speakers, so this whole branch of linguistics was fatally skewed from the off. Nobody (it would seem) has ever questioned whether these 'Goidelic' languages, as we might call them (Welsh, Cornish, Breton, Gaelic), were even Indo-European, much less of the Western European branch of that fertile tree. And of course the pre-historians have taken at complete face value the 'fact' that the Goidelics and the Celts are all one people. I know this is hard to credit, but that's really what happened. That's the way academic paradigms get built. From the downright silly upwards.

So who exactly were the Celts? The Celts were probably Iron Age German-speakers – whether a tribe or a war-band or even an organisation it's difficult to say – who appeared to operate on two levels: as a trading outfit specialising in metals and as a conquering army. They were either the originators or the chief distributors of the La Tène style of metalwork (that's the stuff with all the curly designs). The Celts latterly set up states, though not very successful ones since they lacked writing. These states included the Gaulish ones in France and northern Italy that the Romans later defeated; and which the Romans ruled on exactly the same basis as the Celts, i.e. as a tiny ruling elite governing the existing aboriginal population, though in their case with rather more success since they had a bureaucracy. The Goidelics, meanwhile, operated much the same kind of system in the British Isles. Only the far west of

Britain and Ireland was actually settled by a majority Goidelic population, but they ruled over the rest of the British Isles – with its English-speaking aboriginal population. The two cultures did come together in one area, northern France, which is where an expanding German-speaking culture comes closest to an expanding Goidelic one. Hence the Druids, the intellectual class of the Goidelics, are known to have been operating in Gaul, where they came into contact with the La Tène style and took it home with them. When the Romans drove the Druids out of Gaul and Britain (it may even have been that the Romans invaded Britain to extirpate Druid meddling in Gaul), the Druids retreated to Ireland, where they adopted Christianity but made sure it was *Goidelic* Christianity (what we nowadays call *Celtic* Christianity) rather than the Roman variety adopted by the rest of Western Europe. Hence, when the rest of Western Europe was being plunged into the Dark Age, the Irish Goidelics were able to stay immune and then start, in the guise of anti-Roman Christianity, what we know as the Celtic Revival of the 7th, 8th and 9th centuries which finally polished off the Roman Catholic theocracy and launched Modern Europe into (well, finally) outer space. Well done, the Irish! Kick the Pope!

But back to the French. Scholars' insistence that they originally spoke a 'Celtic' language (their term for a language akin to Welsh, Breton, Cornish, Scots Gaelic etc., and a term that we will continue to use since that is, alas, what most readers will find familiar), means that the French must have undertaken a rather formidable triple language shift. They start off speaking Celtic, within a few centuries they've all switched over to a completely different language, Latin, and within a few centuries more they're speaking a third language, French. The southern French might add that they've had to make four changes, since most of them used to speak Occitan but now speak French. (*Occitan* is the now politically-correct term for what we used to call *Provençal* or *Languedoc* so, ever-anxious not to offend, I will adopt the term here.) But the French, as they never cease pointing out to us, are an outstandingly intellectual race, well capable of taking any number of language shifts in their stride. Why they should want to go through such a vexatiously inconvenient process is quite another question, but the French, as we British never cease pointing out to them, are an outstandingly silly race.

My own view, for what it's worth, is that originally the French spoke French, but switched over to French at some point during their time in the Roman Empire, subsequently adopting French under Frankish rule before finally settling on French in modern times. The only language shift of any note is that the people of southern France gradually went over from Occitan to the northern dialect under the growing cultural and political dominance of Paris, just as the people of north Britain adopted southern English under the growing cultural and political dominance of London. Oh yes, and of course the French/Celtic language cline in Brittany moved gradually but inexorably westwards, just as the English/Celtic language cline did in Cornwall, Wales, Scotland and Ireland. So the French aren't half as smart as they think they are, nor half as stupid as we think they are. In fact they're just the same as us. What a horrible thought.

But the status of 'Gaulish' (i.e. the language of ordinary French people in pre-Roman times) might allow a convenient opportunity for a set-piece battle between Applied Epistemology and Academic Orthodoxy. Since we believe '*What is* is *what was* unless there's clear evidence that it wasn't', we're pretty much obliged to believe that the Gauls spoke French; whereas orthodoxy equally fervently believes that 'History is an endless story of derring-do and frenzied change whenever the evidence allows of that possibility', which has led them to assume as a more or less self-evident fact that the Gauls spoke a Celtic language, presumptively very similar to Welsh. That's clear enough: French or Welsh? So what's the battlefield terrain like? Treacherous but passable:

1. Whatever language the Gauls spoke, it was unwritten and therefore there can't be direct clinching evidence one way or the other.

2. The few pre-Roman or non-Roman inscriptions found in France deal with things like calendar months and proper names which are not normally couched in demotic terms (our own months, for instance, are Latin).

3. These inscriptions are written in either Latin or Greek characters and therefore will tend to be transcribed into these languages, whatever the original.

4. These inscriptions occasionally refer to things like Beltane and Moon goddesses which we associate with our own Celtic fringe (though that connection is itself highly arguable).

5. We don't know for sure whether the 'Gauls' were the ordinary French population or a foreign warrior caste.

They might conceivably be a Celtic-speaking elite who came from Britain.

6. There is definitely a 'Welsh'-speaking population living in western Gaul in modern historic times (i.e. the Bretons of Brittany). We don't know how far east this population extended in Roman times. We don't know even whether it existed at all in Roman times, since early historians speak of the Bretons being British Celts transplanted during the Dark Ages.

7. At various times, parts of Gaul fell under the sway of people who spoke neither Latin nor Welsh, viz. Greeks, Carthaginians, Germans, all of whom may be assumed to have left some evidence of their passing and generally stirred the ancient language pot.

But the one factor that dwarfs everything else is:

8. It's an agreed fact that there was one class of highly educated people operating throughout Gaul at the relevant time, and that was the Druids. And it's overwhelmingly likely that they spoke Welsh. So *any* 'Welsh' traces in ancient France can be ascribed to them and not the general population.

So what to make of all this? One thing is for sure: to say dogmatically that the ordinary inhabitants of France spoke a 'Celtic' language related to Welsh is just plain wrong, and academic historians should be thoroughly ashamed of themselves for doing so. But there's nothing here to allow any counter-dogmatism about them speaking French either. So, as usual, we must turn to the 'non-historical' sources to decide, which in Applied Epistemological terms means exploring common-sense deductions and, above all, the anomalies.

The geographical expression 'Gauls' was used by the Romans to cover three distinct peoples:

the Cis-Alpine Gauls (of northern Italy);

the Trans-Alpine Gauls (of Provence);

the Hither Gauls (in the rest of France).

And these were, it seems, bounded by people speaking quite different languages:

the Germans (in Germany);

the Helvetians (in Switzerland);

the Belgae (in Flanders);

the Aquitanians (in south-western France).

Now of course, since Caesar's time, everybody has moved around, triple-shifted languages and generally been subject to various Dark Age melting pots, but, by a truly staggering set of coincidences, these people seem somehow to have managed to re-assemble themselves in a strangely familiar language pattern. The 'Gauls' are still divided into the three areas they occupied in Classical times, and are still speaking three variants of the same language:

the Cis-Alpine Gauls of northern Italy nowadays speak Italian;

the Trans-Alpine Gauls of Provence speak (spoke) Occitan;

the Hither Gauls in the rest of France speak French.

And they are still bounded by people speaking quite different languages:

the Germans are still speaking German;

the Helvetians are still (just about) speaking Romansch;

the Belgae are still speaking Dutch;

the Aquitanians of south-western France are still speaking Basque.

So, you takes your choice. Either orthodoxy is correct and we have a gigantic set of coincidences, or Applied Epistemology is correct and everyone is more or less exactly where they always were. *Asterix Stays at Home* ... not a big seller.

A number of modern languages claim to be derived from Latin, the main ones being Italian, French, Spanish, Portuguese, Occitan, Catalan and Romanian. This is scarcely surprising by the standards of National Creation Myth-making, since Latin has the two very best credentials: highly prestigious and safely dead. In terms of cold, hard, historic fact, it's certainly true that the chief purveyors of Latin to the unlettered – the Roman Empire and the Catholic Church – really were politico-cultural behemoths that dominated Europe for centuries. But is it cold, hard, historic fact that, between them, these two fine institutions gave most of Western Europe and a blob of Eastern Europe their languages? Let's start by clearing Romanian out of the way. Or rather let us allow a quorum of non-Romanian linguists to clear Romanian out of the way by agreeing with them that

a) Romanian is quite differently structured to Latin;

b) Romania was at best a marginal part of the Roman Empire;

c) Romanians are notoriously prone to make exaggerated claims for pseudo-cultural antecedents of all kinds.

Romanian linguists might, if they were feeling particularly waspish, point out that very much the same could be said substituting 'Parisians' or 'Portuguese', but forbear to do so, no doubt on the principle of hanging together or hanging separately. But let us leave these internal linguistic spats to one side and consider the origin of the Romance (Romance = 'Western European languages derived from Roman, i.e. Latin') languages proper and *en tout*. We know the drill: a) absolute glaring anomalies; and b) a complete unawareness on the part of the relevant academics that any of the anomalies even exist.

Anomaly One: Plus Ça Change

A language is such a vast agglomeration of words and grammar, and is spoken by so many different individuals, that it cannot help but be in a constant process of change. On the other hand, since there's the need to communicate between these individuals, there's also a strong countervailing tendency to ensure that these changes are kept to a kind of uniform minimum. In modern times, both these processes have been accelerated because technical advance both requires a constant diet of neologisms, and provides the means – compulsory education and the mass media – to ensure a reasonable uniformity. English, for example, can be spoken as a mother-tongue by hundreds of millions of people on six continents while remaining recognisably the same language for all. In former times the forces making for uniformity were much less, though in parallel the forces for change were much less also, with the net result that local dialects abounded but full language differentiation occurred only when political division or clear geographical barriers interposed.

Since language morphology is such a highly chaotic business, it follows that when full language differentiation does occur (i.e. when complete mutual incomprehensibility is attained), languages that were once the same or merely regional dialects of one another must drift further and further apart over time in an unpredictable and multivariate manner. There's no mechanism we know of that would allow two such languages to evolve side-by-side in the same direction, because any innovation – in grammar, syntax, vocabulary, pronunciation – will be specific to one language and will not occur in the other language. The two languages must over time become more and more different, in more and more different ways.

But tracing language lineages is assisted because

a) every language is an offspring of another language and carries with it most of its predecessor, making the link reasonably obvious from internal linguistic evidence;

b) since generally the people speaking the offspring language will be just over the next range of mountains, geographical propinquity is a decent guide to language relatedness;

c) people en masse have a marked tendency to stay right where they are over centuries and millennia;

d) folks are very attached to their language and it takes rather a lot to get them to give it up.

So all in all, plotting languages, deciphering their lineage, assessing their relationships is, if not an exact science, at least a rational proposition. The Romance languages demonstrate these general principles extremely well. This is a schematic of the geographical pattern of Romance language-speakers today:

FRENCH

CATALAN   OCCITAN

PORTUGUESE   SPANISH   ITALIAN

The linguistic evidence mirrors the geography with great precision: Portuguese resembles Spanish more than any other language; French resembles Occitan more than any other; Occitan resembles Catalan, Catalan resembles Spanish and so forth. So which was the Ur-language? Can't tell; it could be any of them. Or it could be a language that has long since disappeared. *But the original language cannot have been Latin.* All the Romance languages, even Portuguese and Italian, resemble one another more than any of them resemble Latin, and do so by a wide margin. If the position really were as the various national creation myths insist it was, i.e.:

Portuguese   French
        \   /
         \   /
Spanish —— LATIN —— Italian
         /   \
        /   \
   Catalan   Occitan

… it would mean that all six languages managed to defy logic by evolving chaotically in different directions and ending up in the same place, i.e. all being more like one another than their common starting point.

This is so obvious that even the dullards in the Academy (the Académie Française in this case) have shifted about for some kind of explanation (not that any of them actually understand the problem in these terms). One that's punted around in a vague sort of way is to suppose that the evolution of today's Romance languages was by no means random or chaotic. It was *guided*. This kind of thing does occur in a modest kind of way; for example, the Académie Française itself tries to ensure that Modern French travels along a particular route rather than the way most modern languages move when left to their own devices, which is by the wholesale incorporation of English words and usages. But any sort of 'guiding hand' theory runs up against the fact that the only bodies with any kind of clout at the time were the Latin authorities (either the Empire or the Church) which makes them unfortunate choices for the orderly gallop *away* from Latin. But perhaps it was all done on a much more informal basis, since it's true that intensive cultural interchange can lead to small-scale language parallelisms ('I see the Italians have dropped that rather absurd neuter gender from Latin, Jean-Claude, why don't we do the same?'), though the notion of the Dark Ages as a period of intensive cultural interchange is a bit rich even for my revisionist tastes.

So nowadays, a rather better dodge has been offered into evidence: 'vulgar Latin'. This is our old friend *the cut-out* in a new guise, and it certainly solves the immediate problem, because now the evolutionary language-tree can be put into its traditional and scientifically acceptable form:

Latin

Vulgar Latin

Portuguese   Spanish   Catalan   Provençal   French   Italian

There *was* a language around at the time that was a kind of stripped-down Latin used by the polyglot Roman army (and presumably more widely) – Dog Latin or Soldier's Latin – but the problem here is that 'stripped-down Latin' is absolutely nothing like the kind of 'proto-Romance' that's needed. Latin is already simpler than any Romance language, so a simplified version is further still from the Romance languages, not closer. There is also another language, some traces of which survive, which *does* qualify as a 'proto-Romance' (not surprisingly, since it is in fact early written Italian), and by combining the attributes of these two known languages, the palaeolinguists and their running dogs from the History and Classics departments have cobbled together a theory that all of them find eminently satisfying.

But now it's time to introduce you to another gambit from the Hide-the-Anomaly playbook. This one is The Positive Benefits of Negative Evidence. As you will know by now, historians are not allowed to make things up as they go along; they have to base every statement on a piece of contemporaneous documentation. So when there's no contemporaneous documentation there can be no history. Were you to ask a historian of the later Roman Empire, 'Can you tell me how and when this "vulgar Latin" spread through the western Empire so that it could later on evolve into the modern Romance languages?', you would be firmly told: 'I'd love to, but unfortunately there isn't any contemporary documentation and, as you know, I'm not allowed to speculate in its absence.' 'Why isn't there any contemporary documentation?' 'It was an unwritten language.' And everyone's off the hook.

But let us do what the academics ought to have done, and reconstruct the circumstances that *must have happened in order for the orthodox version to be true*:

1. The people of Spain, Portugal, France and northern Italy are speaking one or more Celtic languages related to Welsh.

2. In the period 250 BC to 50 BC, all these areas become part of the Roman Empire and are ruled by people speaking Latin.

3. The process of converting them from their own Celtic languages to Latin begins.

4. Meanwhile, a different language, a kind of amalgam of Latin/Spanish/French/Italian, is evolving somewhere in the Empire.

5. This too starts spreading.

6. Now the ordinary folk have a choice: they can either stick with Latin which is very simplified and gives them full communication to most of their fellows and all the

higher-ups of the ruling class; or they can switch to this new 'vulgar Latin' which is highly complex and allows them to communicate only with 'vulgar Latin' speakers.

7. For some baffling reason, they all choose the latter.

8. For some other baffling reason, nobody in high places thinks to mention in any surviving piece of documentation the quite startling fact that an entire quadrant of the Roman Empire is chattering away in a new language.

9. But they are, and when the Roman Empire in the west comes to an end, this language starts to develop into regional dialects which in turn form the basis of Portuguese, Spanish, Catalan, Occitan, French and Italian.

Wow, that's a story worth writing up. I wonder why nobody has ever got round to doing so. Oh yes, that's right, it's because there's no contemporaneous documentation.

Anomaly Two: The Latin Quarter

The Roman Empire extended from Glasgow to the Persian Gulf, from Marrakesh to the Ukraine. This area varied between some of the most civilised and culturally advanced parts of the Earth's surface (Mesopotamia, Egypt, Greece, Rome) to some of the most benighted (Glasgow). The degree of Roman influence also varied hugely from one area to another, depending on such things as the length of time within the Empire, military significance, the presence of veterans' colonies and – most important of all – the strength of the indigenous pre-Roman culture. There is, it seems, no general pattern except that – remarkably – one particular corner of the Empire, but only that area, was apparently so thoroughly suffused by Roman values that the entire population switched over from their existing languages to Latin (and then evolved their Latin into Italian, French, Spanish, Portuguese, etc.). So let us once more sketch in the arena for dispute between Orthodoxy and Applied Epistemology. It would be fair to say that the former doesn't regard this as a problem in the first place. As far as orthodoxy is concerned, it's a night-follows-day proposition that certain backward areas – i.e. ones without an existing culture based on a written language – would be so thoroughly suffused with the new Roman civilisation that they would give up their existing language and switch over to Latin (or one of its variants). This is clearly unsustainable, for the following reasons:

1. It occurred only in one contiguous area – Italy, France, Iberia – but not in others – Britain, the Low Countries, the Rhineland, Austria, Hungary, the Balkans – that were even less civilised.

2. Nor can the general area Italy–France–Iberia really be said to be 'uncivilised', since large swathes of it had already been occupied by Etruscans, Greeks and Carthaginians.

3. We have no reason to believe that being less civilised in the sense of having no written language makes a local population more susceptible to having their language changed.

Is there, then, something peculiar about this corner of the

Empire that would make it particularly susceptible to Latin influence? Not on the face of things: parts of it – for example, Latium – were Roman for upwards of a thousand years; other parts of it – for example, northern France – were conquered late and deserted early; hardly any of it was of great military significance, though, oddly, nearby bits that *were* militarily significant like the Rhineland, northern Britain, Pannonia, Illyria, etc. didn't succumb to Latinisation. Frankly, it's completely baffling why, say, the French and the Spanish should adopt Latin whereas the Flemings and the Basques decided not to. Of course it's perfectly possible that this is just 'one of those things that happen in history', but it's up to orthodoxy to explain carefully why, say, London (under Latin-speaking control from c. 50 AD to c. 500 AD) should decline to be Romancified, whereas Paris (under Latin-speaking control for the same length of time, c. 50 BC to 400 AD) should do so with enthusiasm. It's only Applied Epistemologists in fact who can claim that no explanation is called for, because they believe that Parisians were already Romance-speaking when the Romans arrived, whereas Londoners were not.

It also goes without saying that the Romans anticipated the Anglo-Saxons' language imposition programme by always stopping short in order to leave Celtic-speakers on the western margins. We are, it seems, once again in the presence of the weirdly flexible Celtic language cline. Since nobody has ever suggested that the Romans went in for Anglo-Saxon-style ethnic cleansing, it follows, if the accepted version is true, that the various local populations must have switched over from Celtic to Latin on the gradualist basis of individual choice, that over several centuries the 'metropolitan' language slowly displaced the local patois because individuals started to prefer Latin as the more useful language, whenever the opportunity presented. The question that unavoidably arises is: 'When did the opportunity present?' One can just about accept that perhaps the Cis-Alpine Gauls of Milan might embrace Latin with some enthusiasm – they did, after all, fight a long war with Rome for the right to be Roman citizens – but the idea of Portuguese fishermen or stone-cutters in the Corrèze going Latin is less easy to swallow. It's not, I think, being overly stereotypical to say that such people never change anything very much from one millennium to the next; but even if they felt moved to switch languages, how exactly did they manage to do so? How many Latin-speakers do you suppose a 2nd-century shepherd in the Auvergne is going to come across in the course of his lifetime? What, in your opinion, is the likelihood of him meeting, then marrying, a Latin-speaking shepherdess and raising Latin-speaking children? Apparently they all did.

The conversion of lowly types from one language to another is often portrayed as part of general 'trickle-down theory'. Actually, history doesn't record what the toffs spoke, it records what they *wrote*, and it makes a difference. Even now, there are people who believe that, say, early Irish monks spoke Latin because they left records in Latin. Judging from the language of the surviving records, the Vatican has always had a Classically-trained cleaning staff. But for triggering Romance language-shifts, trickle-down theory has to operate both with great velocity and great circumspection: Tacitus (I think; I have lost the reference) refers to a Spanish nobleman 'coming down to the coast' to learn Latin in the 1st century

AD, which, though a throwaway remark of no consequence to Tacitus, appears to indicate that after three centuries of Roman rule, even the Iberian ruling elite were still speaking the aboriginal language. That doesn't leave much time for

1. the upper classes to learn to speak Latin;

2. Latin to 'trickle down' to everyone else;

3. the conversion of Latin into Castilian, Catalan and Portuguese;

4. the 'fixing' of these languages in order to prevent ...

5. ... a Gothic and then an Arabic trickle-down process starting in the 5th century when the Goths and then the Arabs take over these former Roman provinces.

It could be done – the creation myth demands that it must have been done – but even scholars are obliged to admit that there's no actual evidence that it was done. Which is a shame, because without the clumsy insertion of the creation myth there's no need for any of these historical extravaganzas: it's perfectly natural for a Castilian-speaking nobleman to 'go down to the coast to learn Latin', just as his ancestors would have 'gone down to the coast to learn' Punic and Greek and his successors would go to Toulouse and Cordoba to learn Gothic and Arabic when these were the languages of administration in his country. Come to think of it, Castilian noblemen were still going off to learn Latin in the 16th century when the language of administration in Spain was Latin once more. As a matter of strict fact, the local nobs *still* go off to learn Latin, though the actual languages spoken in the Iberian peninsula (even by the nobs) were, the last time I looked, Portuguese, Castilian, Catalan and Basque. Let's hope that archaeologists rooting through the ruins of Madrid a thousand years hence don't come across a well-preserved Latin primer and start constructing yet more linguistic fantasies.

Anomaly Three: The Gap Years

One of the many things missing in the post-Roman Romance area is literature. In the 600 years or so between the disappearance of the Roman Empire in the west and about 1000 AD, nothing much has survived anywhere in the whole general area of France–Italy–Spain–Portugal except monkish hagiographies, some Church histories, a smattering of annals and a few bureaucratic odds and ends. Why is this? Orthodoxy can't reasonably explain it, which is perhaps why the current trend is to say, 'What Dark Ages?', though this may be more because experts can never stand using a term that everybody else uses. Because it sure as hell was dark compared to the before and after. In the thousand years *before* the Dark Ages, this smallish corner of the Earth's surface was a definite cultural hot-spot: Rome, Syracuse, Etruria, Marseille, Cartagena were right up there alongside China, India, the Middle East and Greece in the world civilisation league. And in the thousand years *after* the Dark Ages, Italy, France, Spain and Portugal have shown a clean pair of heels to the rest of the world.

Between these two periods, for approximately 600 years, everyone lived in trees. This doesn't happen naturally. Someone, somewhere must have been interfering with

Western Europe's natural affinity with civilisation. One explanation might be that the Church, following a Roman imperial precedent, didn't allow vernacular languages to become written languages, but instead operated a scriptural monopoly ensuring that all writing was in Latin and that all writers were, perforce, churchmen. Since the local temporal powers throughout the Dark Ages were Goths, Franks, Vandals, Lombards, etc. who didn't speak the local vernacular languages nor, for the most part, write in their own languages, a mutually beneficial arrangement was entered into by which the Church would support the legitimacy of the temporal rulers (and provide them with a basic clerical administration) while the temporal rulers would enforce the Church's monopoly over all aspects of literacy (not to mention religion). This would explain the otherwise perplexing lack of progress anywhere in Western Europe during the Dark Ages, since a Church monopoly over literacy (and education and administration and jurisprudence and all the civilised arts) could have been practical only in conditions of a very rigid control, over a very limited number of literate individuals. This would have been essential because literacy is so powerful, so useful and so relatively easy to acquire, that unless there is active, constant suppression, it will always expand exponentially, and a widespread literate class is quite incompatible with a steady-state theocracy lasting several centuries. And, it's tempting to say, it's only possible in the long run – and 600 years is an awfully long run – if the language people speak is *not* the language they write.

This tendency is clearly visible in the closing stages of the Roman Empire itself, when the newly dominant Church, aided and abetted by insecure post-Constantine emperors, went in for a frenzy of book-burning and heresy-hunting which seems to have paralysed large sections of the civil administration. The sources are a bit shifty on this point since virtually all of them are Christian, but one can't help noticing that the whole literate world of the late Empire seems to have been obsessed with bizarre scriptural squabbles between schismatics within and without the Pauline Church, while the actual decline and fall of the Roman Empire is noted only as an interesting backdrop. This general situation is familiar enough to our own modern sensibilities, having witnessed the methods of modern totalitarian statecraft, and it appears that the early Church understood very clearly that *all* heresy, however innocent in itself, must be crushed at once if political dominance is to be retained indefinitely. The mere act of independent thought will, over time – over quite short a time – create unstoppable fissures in the totalitarian structure. The idea that the Church kept the flame of civilisation alive during the Dark Ages is something between a sick joke and the Big Lie.

But that's only my opinion. Orthodoxy (academic as well as religious) holds that everybody throughout Italy, France, Spain and Portugal as they embarked on the Dark Ages was speaking a *written* language, Latin, so none of the above applies. They don't explain how, as Latin 'evolved' into Italian, French, Spanish, etc., the local monkish candidates managed to cope with the fact that the language they learned at their mother's knee was imperceptibly differentiating itself from the language they were writing in the monastery, though it would have provided a novel twist for contemporary kitchen-sink dramatists ('Eh, mither, that lad wi' his fancy education and old-fashioned talk …'). Obviously, some completely different explanation is called for in order to account for the striking fact that nothing culturally happened for six centuries in a region that was a world cultural power-house before the Dark Age and again immediately after it. Not unexpectedly, Western historians do have an *un*reasonable explanation for this curious hiatus, and it has been taught to everybody for so many centuries that it has taken on the patina of being self-evident. However, roughly 30 seconds' actual examination reveals it to be the purest horse manure.

In essence, they say, there was a never-ending succession of comings-and-goings of various unlettered barbarians, and that the consequent mayhem and rapine didn't allow for anything very much in the way of the civilised arts. Sounds plausible, but let's just check out the theory with, say, France. Now, French history *after* 1000 AD is well documented: it's a never-ending succession of comings-and-goings by Normans, English, Spaniards, Prussians, Austrians, Russians, Germans; it's a *mélange* of mayhem and rapine as *apanage* disputes, religious strife and civil wars are interspersed with *jacqueries*, *frondes*, *manifestations* and bloody revolution. Result: a thousand years of being a world cultural power-house. During the Dark Ages, by contrast, France was ruled for the whole period by the Merovingian and Carolingian Franks, in unbroken and mostly peaceful succession, said regime being – in so far as we can judge from the admittedly scanty and biased sources – strong enough throughout to ensure a reasonable degree both of internal tranquillity and external security. Result: not even the cuckoo clock. Still, it's a good theory because everybody believes it – and *that*, as the Church will tell you, is the crucial ingredient of a good theory.

Oddly, wherever and whenever the Church's dominance *was* challenged anywhere in the Romance area – in Spain and Portugal by the Arabs, in northern France by the Normans, in Provence by the Cathars and the Septimanian Jews, in Italy during the struggle between the Guelphs and Ghibellines – three things occurred:

1. vernacular literatures suddenly appeared;

2. culture took off like a rocket;

3. everyone stopped triple-shifting languages and instead carried right on speaking the ones they'd got.

And have done from that day to this. *Incroyable mais vrai.*

Anomaly Four: Latin As She Is Wrote

So where, precisely, does Latin fit into all this? Here we have another linguistic mystery. Although it's true that Latin is grammatically and syntactically very far distant from any of the present-day Romance languages, Latin does have a remarkably similar vocabulary to all of them. This precise concordance is in fact the origin of the Creation Theory itself.

Q: How do you know French is derived from Latin?

A: Because most of the words in French also appear in Latin, so there must be a causal connection.

Q: How do you know that it wasn't French that caused Latin?

A: Because Latin is much earlier than French.

Q: Oh, right.

Actually the correct question, though it's never posed and never answered, is: 'How can Language A be grammatically and syntactically distant from Language B and yet share a vocabulary with it?' To which the correct answer is: 'Well, this can't happen in the natural state of language morphology because as soon as Language A and Language B come into existence – i.e. are spoken with mutual unintelligibility by two different populations – then they must drift apart in a chaotic fashion, with vocabulary moving apart at roughly the same rate as the grammar and syntax. So this is not a "natural situation".'

However, this particular type of language development does occur in, as it were, the natural world, in the case of pidgins – when a polyglot population (normally of slaves or something similar) is suddenly thrown together and is obliged to learn the 'master' language. I suppose if you were to stretch the case (and orthodoxy is known to stretch the case when *in extremis*) you might try to mount a case for the entire populations of Italy, France, Spain and Portugal developing a Romance pidgin, based on Latin, that subsequently evolved into Italian, French, Spanish, etc., but nobody has suggested this (yet). Fortunately, there's a much more reasonable explanation that meets all the facts: Latin is not a natural language. When written, Latin takes up approximately half the space of written Italian or written French (or written English, German or any natural European language). Since Latin appears to have come into existence in the first half of the first millennium BC, which was the time when alphabets were first spreading through the Mediterranean basin, it seems a reasonable working hypothesis to assume that Latin was originally a shorthand compiled by Italian speakers for the purposes of written (confidential? commercial?) communication. This would explain:

a) the very close concordance between Italian and Latin vocabulary;

b) the conciseness of Latin in, for instance, dispensing with separate prepositions, compound verb forms and other 'natural' language impedimenta;

c) the unusually formal rules governing Latin grammar and syntax;

d) the lack of irregular, non-standard usages;

e) the unusual adoption among Western European languages of a specifically vocative case ('Dear Marcus, re. your letter of …').

But if this were the case, if Latin were originally a written shorthand, is it likely that people would actually start speaking it? Does this not conjure up visions of shorthand-typists, left for several generations on a desert island, eventually beginning to converse in Pitman's? It would indeed be a ludicrous proposition, except that we actually possess historical records of a Mediterranean people learning to converse in a hitherto written language and managing to do so without difficulty in a single generation: the Israelis, with Hebrew, in the middle of the 20th century. Both the Ancient Romans and the modern Israelis were able to develop cohesive, aggressive and expansionist new states amidst a sea of hostile neighbours, and it must be assumed that the unique language played some part in this. It goes beyond the scope of this book, but there are good reasons to believe that the possession of a written language (and more especially the development of artificial languages for the purpose of writing) is the key to understanding the whole of Ancient History. Hebrew and Latin will in time be recognised alongside Old Norse, Classical Greek, Sanskrit, Punic, Sumerian Cuneiform, Egyptian hieroglyphs and other 'non-demotic' languages as being essentially cultural artefacts adopted for a purpose, and not, as linguists insist, merely the surviving record of what ordinary people spoke.

* * *

As with the question of Anglo-Saxon and English, we have once again some wildly variant history, but that departs from the mainstream only depending on how one answers the narrow question: Did the Romance languages come from Latin or did Latin come from a Romance language? Nothing in the annals of history is changed, however this question is answered; though everything is changed in the telling of history itself. So, whom to ask? Whom to consult on this intriguing but technical historico-cultural-linguistic poser? Why, Classicists, of course. And there are plenty of them to consult because Latin, as the supposed root language of most of Western Europe, is intensively studied throughout Western Europe. Ah yes, it's the old turkeys-voting-for-Christmas conundrum. Or as the Classicists would put it: *Quis custodiet ipsos custodes?*

CHAPTER FOUR

As Above, So Below

And so finally to the oddest, least reported anomaly of all: the Latinate content of English. First, some rough-hewn numbers. According to the latest *OED* figures, English has about 700,000 words, which is in itself rather staggering because the usual number bandied around for other European languages is 50,000. Though, as usual, the even more staggering fact is that nobody seems to think that this incredibly anomalous position requires any explanation beyond the somewhat airy: 'Oh well, you have to remember English is an amalgam of other European languages.' Strewth, how many languages? Still, the official version of the actual amalgam present in English is:

two-thirds Germanic ('derived from Anglo-Saxon')

one-third Latinate ('derived from Latin and French')

But this has to be somewhat tempered by the fact that quite a lot of English words are either of unknown origin or are known to be of recent coinage, made up more or less on the spot to cover the quite extraordinary ingress of novelties following the Scientific and Industrial Revolutions (many, of course, down to English-speakers who therefore get the naming rights). So, let's err on the side of caution, and assume there are 100,000 words of Latinate origin in English.

First of all, is there a problem? Is the fact that English is an ostensibly Germanic language, but contains 100,000 words derived from the non-Germanic languages of Latin and French, something that requires an explanation? Or should we shrug it off as just one of those crazy things that happen in history? This *is* in fact the official explanation, which argues that English, as it developed from Old English (i.e. Anglo-Saxon) through Middle English to Modern English, picked up a vast number of new words from a variety of Latinate sources – the new Norman administration, the Catholic Church, continental cultural influences generally – to reflect the new and somewhat enlightened circumstances of England after 1066. In support of this argument, it's often pointed out that Latinate English words tend to be used in more sophisticated ways than Germanic English words, the usual example quoted being that words for animals (*pig*, *cow*, *sheep*) are Germanic, but the words for their meat (*pork*, *beef*, *mutton*) are Latinate. This general belief is now so firmly enshrined in English consciousness that the very lowest form of English, swear-words, are actually referred to as 'Anglo-Saxon language'. Though swear-words themselves aren't in agreement with this view: *shit*, *fuck*, *arse* and *bugger* are Germanic; *cunt*, *damn*, *balls* and *sod* are Latinate.

All very fascinating, but is it true? Did these Latinate words come from French and Latin? To help decide the question, let's compare English with the other main non-Romance Western

European language, German. The two aren't *very* comparable in the sense that German has a decidedly small Latinate content, but let's at any rate consider which of them has the closer relationship to potential Latinate sources:

1. Western and southern Germans were in the Roman Empire for several centuries; no Anglo-Saxons were.

2. Most Germans were within the Frankish Empire for several centuries; Anglo-Saxon England was not.

3. Germany and Anglo-Saxon England became converted to Roman Christianity at roughly the same time.

4. England was ruled by French-speaking Normans for several centuries; Germany was not.

Given these facts, which side had more Latinate exposure? It's hard to say because there doesn't seem much in it, though it's not hard to say that for one set of influences to produce 100,000 Latinate words and the other a few hundred would, were a paradigm not involved, be considered entirely ridiculous.

But perhaps Germans are peculiarly immune to linguistic hybridisation (except Anglo-Saxon Germans, of course), so a better comparison-language might be Welsh. This too has a relatively small Latinate content, but has had a Latinate exposure conditioned by the fact that

1. All Welsh-speakers were in the Roman Empire for several centuries.

2. The Welsh were converted to Roman Christianity at about the same time as Anglo-Saxon England, and both remained so for the next thousand years.

3. Roughly half of Welsh-speakers were ruled by French-speaking Normans, the other half were not.

Much the same situation: the relationship to Latinate sources seems entirely comparable, but again the Welsh seem bafflingly immune to whatever it was that was afflicting the Anglo-Saxons. Perhaps they ate less meat.

What, then, are the rules about word-derivation? All languages – except presumably the first – are derived from other languages, so it follows that most of the words in any given language are derived from another language. If Language B is derived from Language A, then it is to be expected that virtually all the words of Language B will either be the same as, or corruptions of, or evolved versions of words in Language A ('cognate with' in the jargon). Generally speaking, we have no direct historical evidence of the actual relationship between languages, partly because most of the changes happened pre-historically and partly because early historical sources don't overly concern themselves with matters of language. (The philological industry, significantly or not, is a largely 19th-century Anglo-German invention.) Hence linguists are obliged to use the evidence contained within the languages themselves – essentially the degree to which cognates are present – to work out which language gave rise to which.

Since language-change is a chaotic business to begin with, ascribing provenance is a slightly hit-and-miss affair; but to compound linguists' difficulties, there's one critical structural problem that can never be satisfactorily overcome: *although a large number of cognates shared between two languages points to their being derived from the same language, this cannot of itself demonstrate which language gave rise to which.* Were we, for instance, to be presented with parallel texts in Papuan New Guinea pidgin and English, we might observe that they have a great many cognates and that therefore the two languages must be closely related, but we wouldn't immediately be in a position to decide whether

a) the Papuan pidgin was derived from English; or

b) English was derived from the Papuan pidgin; or

c) both languages were derived from some third language.

In this case, historical evidence does allow us to sort the matter out, because we have firm evidence that English-speakers occupied Papua New Guinea and reported the local language situation, which didn't include any quasi-English vocabulary. But we must take care that the historical evidence is not back-constructed from lazy linguistic assumptions or vice versa. It is improper to assume that English is derived from Anglo-Saxon or that French is derived from Latin just because of the undoubted fact that Anglo-Saxon- and Latin-speakers occupied those countries. Unfortunately for our purposes, neither the Anglo-Saxons nor the Romans recorded the local language situation when they arrived.

Into this *mélange* of cause-and-effect we have to throw the further complication of *loan-words*, words or phrases of one language adopted by the speakers of another language. This is a notorious minefield, but one that has to be trodden because, while cognates indicate language-relatedness, loan-words do not, and there's no absolute way of telling them apart. Let me offer an illustration of the problems that can arise: *yoghurt*. Now, this is often stated to be the only Mongolian word in common English usage, but this might in fact be one of the 'urban myths' that afflict all matters of etymology. Why is etymology so prone to such 'imprecisions'? That's easy: there are 700,000 words in the English language, so no one word gets a huge amount of analysis and anything halfway reasonable is likely to get entered into the lists. Here are a few possible sources for *yoghurt* imprecisions:

1. Neither Mongolian orthography nor vowel sounds and consonants are the same as in English, so the English word 'yoghurt' is likely to be only a loose approximation of the Mongolian word for the same milk product.

2. It's unlikely that the word was loaned directly from Mongolian into English. It may well have passed through Hindi, Farsi, German, Italian, Turkish, Greek, etc. on the way. And of course it may have started in one of these intermediate languages and gone t'other way to Mongolian.

3. It's perfectly possible, though admittedly unlikely, that Mongolian loaned the word from English! The Mongols, after all, reached Central Europe in the 13th century; and since milk and milk products are a common feature of both countries' cuisines, it cannot be excluded that the Mongols took the substance and the word back home with them. (And *yogh* is, according to orthodoxy, an obsolete Middle English letter.) It's true that, if so, the word *yoghurt* appears to have dropped out of English usage in the meantime, but that too happens all the time.

4. 'Yoghurt' was coined by the Express Dairies in the 1950s and was deliberately designed by them to evoke Central Asian origins.

When dealing with 700,000 words in a world where every language is related in some degree to every other language – English and Mongolian are both members of the Indo-European/Altaic/Semitic super-family – and in which cultural exchanges are going on at every level, in every direction, during both recorded and unrecorded time, in written and unwritten form, it's essential not to take even the most confident assertions by linguists at face value. They're often right, but when they're wrong, they're very, very wrong.

Loan-words usually arise when Culture B imports some novelty from Culture A and, since by definition there can't be an existing word for it in Culture B's language, either a neologism is coined or, more sensibly, Culture A's word for that novelty is imported too – with a suitable adjustment of spelling and pronunciation to make it comfortable for B-speakers. Like *yoghurt*, for instance. It may not sit entirely comfortably on the English tongue, but it beats *bacterio-milk solid*. This situation can arise in three ways:

1. By way of trade – in which case the loan-words are quite few.

2. Occupation by people speaking a foreign language – rather more loan-words.

3. Occupation by people speaking a foreign language who introduce 'civilisation' – even more loan-words.

In each case there is a word common to Languages A and B. But in each case there is the possibility that it was Language A that got the word from Language B. After all, invaders find novelties when they occupy foreign lands as well as introducing them. We know this very well from our own contemporary experiences, but when it comes to ancient history we have a marked tendency to forget that the strong borrow from the weak.

Applied Epistemology pays special attention to these kinds of situations, when cause-and-effect can be thoroughly muddied. When first a paradigm is put together, a connected sequence of events has to be constructed. By the nature of the newly-discovered, this sequence is at first simply hypothesised and the theory stands and falls by whether or not these links can later be hardened into chains of evidence. But the Academy is not a Court of Law. What actually happens is that a sequence is hypothesised, some evidence is produced which seems to fall into roughly the right places, the theory is accepted as being provisionally true, it's taught to undergraduates, these undergraduates teach the theory in their turn, and within a generation or two what was provisionally true becomes for all practical purposes self-evidently true. If it happens to be false, then of course the anomalies start to pop up; but, when the paradigm is held to be self-evidently true, these really are regarded as 'anomalies', i.e. something to be explained by reference to a more detailed understanding of how the paradigm works, not as indications that the paradigm itself is wrong.

But how can careful scholars allow the supporting evidence 'to fall roughly into the right places' if the basic paradigm is wrong to start with? This is because cause-and-effect has a built-in structural flaw. When the cause and the effect are put round the wrong way, then all the true evidence still fills the space in between. For instance, when all the people beavering away at the *Oxford English Dictionary* believe that English is derived from Anglo-Saxon and that Anglo-Saxon is derived from German, then hundreds of thousands of English words get given 'from the Old English' and 'from the German' as their derivation. So, when you ask, 'What is the evidence that English is a Germanic language?', you will be told: 'Well, hundreds of the best-qualified people have spent years amassing several hundred thousand examples of English words deriving from German words.' Only an Applied Epistemologist would say: 'We now have several hundred thousand pieces of evidence, compiled by the best-qualified people in the world, that demonstrates our contention that German is derived from English.' Not that an Applied Epistemologist would say that precisely. Rather: 'If the nexus between English and Anglo-Saxon is broken, we have no evidence about the age of English. Nor do we have any evidence about the age of German. Until further and better particulars become available, it is incumbent upon us to be agnostic on the question of which gave rise to which.'

This reversal of cause and effect lies at the heart of many false academic paradigms, going right back to the earliest one about whether God-makes-Man or vice versa. In Applied Epistemology it's known as the Academic Three Card Trick. The Three Card Trick (Find The Lady) is one of the hoariest of conjuring tricks – you can still see it being played out on the streets of tourist London – and involves the conman/conjuror showing the audience three playing-cards, two plain ones and the Queen of Diamonds, which he places face down on the table without apparently altering them in any way, whereupon the audience is invited to bet on which one is the Queen. Since they've just seen the Queen turned over, they point to it and lose their money. The academic version is more, but not very much more, sophisticated and involves the three components of cause-and-effect: the cause, the effect and the causal connection (the last being the Queen of Diamonds). This is how the academic version of the trick is played: both the *cause* and the *effect* parts of any given situation are normally right out in the open, to be measured, labelled and written up in a thousand monographs; the 'and' bit, the *causal connection*, the Queen of Diamonds, is hidden from view, in the sense of not being at all obvious. Now, having two things in clear view and one that is hidden means that the prestidigitator can proceed in one of two ways:

1. turn the Queen face-up, thereby focusing the audience's attention on the causal connection, then surreptitiously switching round the cause and the effect;

2. turn the middle card face-down, thereby persuading the audience that it's the Queen, when in reality there's no causal connection between the other two cards.

We can illustrate the way in which both methods are employed in foisting on the public the illusion about the origins of their spoken language:

1. French and Latin are obviously causally connected because of their common vocabulary, but which gave

rise to which has been switched round, as we shall see;

2. Anglo-Saxon and English lie very close together – the two peoples lived in the same country for centuries, the languages are linguistically related – so they 'must' be causally related.

(Please note – no charge of impropriety is here directed at academics, who are merely unwitting victims of their anxiety to please. They aren't clever enough to actually devise the trick.)

The Three Card Trick pervades the whole of academic life, but history is peculiarly susceptible in that it's actually built on a principle, chronology, that is a one-way cause-and-effect *excluder*: Event B cannot be the cause of Event A if it occurred *after* A. Given the powerful impetus of chronology, history can actually exist without the causal principle at all – as 'just one damned thing after another' – but history without cause-and-effect is a dull and somewhat pointless exercise (a bit like genealogy, a pastime that human beings unaccountably prefer), so historians are forever, quite properly, editorialising from the raw chronological data set before them. In fact, the profession of historian is one devoted to establishing chronologies and then adding the commentary that the bare chronology cannot provide. So used are historians to this process that they take the chronology for granted, they accept the commentary as a rational discourse on that chronology, and then they start adding their own commentary. Since there can be no 'final truth' with the commentary, the amount of it is determined only by the general interest in the particular subject area. We still don't know the causes of the First World War but, by God, we have a thousand explanations and – it's fair to say – a better understanding of the causes of the First World War.

But of course all the commentary is dependent on the chronology being correct. And here's the problem. After a thousand books have appeared, it's doubtful that anybody will go back and check the original documentation to make absolutely sure that Franz Ferdinand was assassinated *before* the outbreak of the war. A thousand books can hardly be wrong. No doubt he was, and no doubt the thousand books have got it right, but what happens when the chronology isn't quite so well documented? What happens when there's *no* chronology? Well, if it happens to be an important moment in history, there might still be a demand for a thousand books; but since history can't be written without a chronology, there must now be a 'best guess' as to what the correct chronology is. Once this best guess is established by peer-review and the teaching of it to succeeding generations of students, we will have a thousand books all containing a possibly incorrect chronology. Now, not only is it unlikely that anybody would think to challenge such a deeply enshrined basic 'fact', but those thousand books will each be full of evidence which *appears to buttress the chronology* because, apart from the odd anomaly, everything in between A and B is between A and B whichever way round the chronology places A and B. Every book will read like a seamless unfolding of events.

But yes, even so, one or two absurdities have to be tacitly accepted for the flaw to remain hidden. If French is a Latinate language, then clearly French must be chrono-logically later than Latin. We have overwhelming evidence of Latin's chronology – the general period 500 BC to 500 AD –

but what is the chronology of the French language? Since we have French inscriptions dating from the 9th century, we know it must have existed as early as the 9th century AD. But history relies on contemporaneous inscriptions for its evidence, thus French began in the 9th century! Probably even historians would accept this as slightly nonsensical if they thought about it, but it's still the answer you will receive from them if you ask. But then, as far as historians are concerned, the origins of the French language isn't a historical question in the first place, it's a linguistic matter. So now watch as the Queen of Diamonds shimmies from place to place:

1. French is assumed to be a Romance language, i.e. derived from Latin.

2. Latin arrived in France with Julius Caesar in the 1st century BC.

3. French is known by contemporary inscriptions to be at least as old as the 9th century AD.

4. A thousand years is long enough for Latin to have evolved into French.

5. No evidence of Latin's evolution into French is available or will ever be available, because the literate classes were writing in pure Latin, and anyway this is all happening in the Dark Ages when nobody is writing much in any language.

Only an Applied Epistemologist would spot the tiny flaw in the argument, the phrase 'at least' in 3.

The fact that there's no *historical* evidence of the French language before the 9th century AD doesn't mean there was no French language before the 9th century AD; it means of course the precise opposite – that the French language must have existed before the 9th century in order to be written down in the 9th century. But this introduces 'bottomless pit syndrome', the curse of all time-based academic disciplines. Human beings find it all but impossible to make sense of anything which has no starting point, so they adopt a 'best guess' one. Nothing wrong with that so long as, once everything is up-and-running, they remember to go back and rub out the fairly arbitrary start point they chose in the first place. But this is tricky because everything they have discovered in the meantime appears to be predicated on the start point, so the start point has in the meantime acquired enormous intellectual clout. It's easier to invent God than to kill him off.

Thus historians have got so used to treating the French language (and indeed the French people) as something that started in the 9th century that they will die at the stake rather than deny it. Or rather they will tie linguists to the stake and wash their hands of the problem. Then it will be the linguists who will die at the stake rather than deny that French is derived from Latin, and hand the problem back to the historians for confirmation that Latin arrived in France in the 1st century BC – otherwise it would be the linguists staring into the bottomless pit of French having no known starting point. And why can't they do that? Well, because if French has no known starting point then it can't be placed after Latin, i.e. it ceases to be a Romance language. And since French is practically the same as all the other Romance languages, that casts them all adrift too. But wait … if the Romance languages have no start point, then they have no place in the Indo-European family tree since, as far as anyone can tell, they might be the *start* of the Indo-European family tree. Actually, there's nothing to stop human language itself being invented on the banks of the Seine, and even Parisians would feel uncomfortable with this degree of primacy. That's the inherent flaw in all theoretical trunk-and-branch systems: you can't go monkeying around in the branches without risking an axe to the trunk.

'Bottomless pit syndrome' affects areas a lot more important than palaeolinguistics. In evolutionary biology, for example, all species are given a chronology based on the earliest known fossil – despite the fact that the existence of the fossil proves only that the species must have existed before then in order to provide palaeontologists with a fossil. Of course, palaeontologists are aware of this *as a fact*, but they take refuge in the assumption: 'Well, let's face it, if it was very much earlier we'd find very much earlier fossils.' Which is fair enough, but even so, we end up in the French situation that the *earliest known fossil* is the *latest possible true date* for a given species. Again, that's fair enough when dealing with trilobites in the Jurassic, because who gives a monkey's about plus or minus a few million years back then? But when it comes to the more pressing matters of the here-and-now, this unacknowledged finagle leads to some sublime nonsense:

1. Most existing species have no fossil record.

2. By virtue of the earliest/latest rule, these are by definition 'young' species.

3. Extinct species always have a fossil record (otherwise we wouldn't know about them).

4. By virtue of the earliest/latest rule, these are by definition 'old' species.

5. Young species are *ex hypothesi* evolved from old species.

6. Therefore presently existing species are the evolved forms of extinct species.

Although it appears to be only common sense that existing species are evolved versions of extinct species, the routine application of this principle across the board gives rise to a persistent assumption among orthodox biologists that *presently existing species are never evolved versions of other presently existing species*. The possibility of this actually being the case – that not a single one of the *n* million presently existing species is the ancestor of another species – is nil, but whether evolutionary biologists (i.e. *all* academic biologists outside Creationist Middle America) are aware of this is not entirely clear. Of course, they know in a theoretical kind of way that there's no earthly reason why the species all around us can't be one another's evolutionary ancestors, but biologists don't like the idea of ancestors walking amongst us any more than the rest of us, so in practice they just ignore the possibility.

If pushed on the point, they would no doubt argue that natural selection makes modern species the *replacement* of extinct species, but if asked why this has turned out to be true in more or less every single case, why we live in a glorious moment of time when natural selection has apparently worked perfectly in *n* million cases, why we can have king crabs and coelacanths but not their *replacements*, why we can have peppered moths and dachshunds happily co-existing with their ancestral breeds but not with their ancestral *species*, why after simulating a billion years of evolution with the fruit-fly we still await a new species, they will engage in violent outbursts of cognitive dissonance.

It's important to know how to deal with academic cognitive dissonance because therein lies the key to successful revisionism. Being an Applied Epistemologist in a land of severely handicapped academics requires careful preparation. Remember that every trained academic – or, more usefully for our purposes, every basic academic textbook – holds all the data you need, arranged in beautifully accessible form, thanks to the need to inculcate that knowledge into every fresh generation of students, and it can be completely relied on thanks to peer-review. All you then have to do is wait for an outburst of cognitive dissonance – or in the case of textbooks, spot an obvious contradiction – and you're away. Asking a biologist to name a currently existing species that has given rise to another currently existing species will normally elicit puzzlement as the hapless expert realises that this seemingly harmless request sets up certain discordances in his brain. He will know that there are n million species to choose from, he will know that hundreds of thousands will presumably qualify; he will also know with juddering certainty that none come swiftly to mind.

What will definitely not happen next is for the biologist to say: 'Good Lord, you've got me there, old chap. What a peculiar lacuna in my training. So peculiar in fact that being as how my professional life is predicated on that training, I must drop everything and investigate the matter.' More likely is: 'Good Lord, is that the time? Must be off. What was the question again? Can't stop. Drop me a line.' Actually, the more thoughtful among them *will* name names – ones you have never heard of, ones with peculiar Latin names drawn from obscure branches of the invertebrates that only trained biologists have the least knowledge of (or can even pronounce). This means, according to these thoughtful evolutionary biologists, that we live in a world where

1. every species you ever heard of is either extinct or non-ancestral;

2. all species that are not extinct but are ancestral happen to be ones you personally have never heard of.

… which is a pretty good piece of mind-reading on their part.

There are various standard gambits for avoiding being blinded by this kind of science. The first is simply to look puzzled, a bit gormless, and say: 'How terribly interesting, I've never heard of that one. Do you have any, you know, better-known examples … er … a bird perhaps or, you know, a mammal …?' This can often be a knockout blow, since his natural reply – 'Listen, pal, cladistics isn't my bag. Look it up on the internet if you're that interested' – is, even to the surliest Life Scientist, a too obviously shifty answer. So he's more likely to come up with something along the lines of: 'Well of course the wolf is ancestral to the dog …'; in which case you should reply, with some firmness because you will be lying: 'Oh really, I thought I read somewhere that most of the experts had rather ruled that out … but of course, you *are* the expert …' This reply works for all examples because there are *no* agreed examples; the hapless biologist will simply be naming something he thinks he remembers from his under-graduate days but actually picked up from Arthur Mee's *Children's Encyclopaedia*. Always bear in mind that at the very highest level – i.e. at the very lowest level of the basic para-digm theory – peer-review often comes down to shared child-hood experiences.

Another good counter is to insist on written evidence. Academics have a reverence for things written down, so while they're quite prepared to lie (in a manner of speaking) while nattering away casually to a layperson, they get terribly nerv-ous if you say: 'Could you jot that down … so I can look it up on the internet?' There generally comes a point when the poor soul refuses to cooperate further. His brain knows quite well what a pickle its owner is in, and starts directing his feet rapidly in the opposite direction. Offer him twenty quid. This always brings him back, since, like the drama critic of the *New York Times*, his professional views are not for sale. Cap his expressions of distaste by making it a hundred … a thousand … start writing a cheque … the results can be hilarious. Or at any rate uproarious.

This impasse is more than a minor piece of dinner party theatre; it has practical applications in the real world of the Life Sciences. Take the following catechism:

1. There are several dozen cat species wandering the Earth right now.

2. They are all remarkably similar to one another (some

can even mate and produce viable, if infertile, off-spring).

3. By the rules of Darwinian Evolution, this means they are all prime candidates for being one another's ancestors.

4. But this is at variance with the 'extinct ancestor' assumption.

5. Therefore all the several dozen present-day cat species 'must have' evolved from an extinct cat species.

Now here's the clever bit. We have reams of information about all the present-day cat species, which means – were they ancestral to one another – we would have a living labora-tory to explore how Darwinian Evolution works (including, of course, *whether* Darwinian Evolution works). But biologists, for some mysterious internal reason of their own, insist that they would much prefer to proceed on the assumption that the common ancestor of all present-day cat species is a *fossil* cat species, i.e. a pile of bones about which we can know very little and which therefore allows us to explore only with the greatest difficulty how Darwinian Evolution works (including whether Darwinian Evolution works).

Now here's the *clever* clever bit. Once it's 'established' that cat evolution is down to fossil bones, the entire matter has to be turned over to the fossil bone experts, the palaeontologists – as opposed to cat zoologists, cat-breeders, cat veterinarians, cat taxidermists, cat-lovers, and a million-and-one interested and knowledgeable observers who may well know a great deal more about cat morphology than the average palaeontologist. (There's not enough that one can say about cat bones to make feline palaeontology a viable specialism in its own right.) But observe the results: now that palaeontologists have been given primacy over all other experts in the field, and since we may take it for granted that palaeontologists are unlikely to question an assumption that gives them such primacy, we can be pretty sure that palaeontologists shall be judge and jury over all questions of cat evolution for evermore. But then palaeontologists are quite used to occupying this position because palaeontology, though a minor subject in itself, happens to be a 'bridging discipline', i.e. one that ensures the integrity of the 'join' between rather more significant branches of learning. Palaeontology acts as the gate-keeper between

the Life Sciences (ruling paradigm: Darwinian Evolution; methodological base: the fossil evidence); and

the Earth Sciences (ruling paradigm: the geological sequence; methodological base: the fossil evidence).

But note that this gate-keeping role is not to prevent the Life Sciences and the Earth Sciences from questioning each others' basic assumptions – that's taken care of by internal academic rules – but to prevent *outsiders* questioning the basic assumptions of either the Life or the Earth Sciences. Everybody knows a fair bit about both animals and rocks, so sticking crowbars in and levering away at contradictions could become a popular sport. But not many of us feel quite so confidently inquisitorial when it comes to fossils. Actually you'd be well advised to steer clear of this particular bridging gap altogether, since it's the methodological base bearing the weight of the whole of the Life and the Earth Sciences, and you wouldn't want that lot falling on you. Unless you're a Creationist of course, in which case you're so thick everything just bounces off. Or an Applied Epistemologist. We actually like the sound of falling masonry.

Now here's the *clever* clever clever bit. With modern techniques, even fossilised bones can be dangerously revealing, so nowadays most professionals have rejected any of the various fossil cat species as the ancestor of the modern cats in favour of a single theoretical 'common ancestral cat', i.e. a fossil species that has not, for some reason, been found yet. You might think a theoretical cat would be hard to study scientifically, but, as Schrödinger pointed out, and as palaeolinguists with their reconstructed languages have discovered, you can build entire academic subjects on such constructs. The process, whether it's a common ancestral species or a common ancestral language, always follows the same pattern:

1. Take all the existing examples (lions, tigers, civets, pussy-cats, etc.; French, Russian, Farsi, Bengali, etc.).

2. Add all the known fossil examples (smilodon, homotherium, miracinonyx, etc.; Latin, Hittite, Sanskrit, etc.).

3. Sieve out the features common to all the examples.

4. Add in anything useful that's common to some of the examples.

5. Select from the result everything that's useful.

6. Remove anything that isn't helpful.

7. Reconstruct the pieces into a whole.

8. Declare the result to be 'the common ancestral cat' or 'proto-Indic'.

9. Put at base of evolutionary table of cats or Indo-European languages.

10. When everybody's grown familiar with the table, remove the quotation marks.

The twin advantage of 'constructs' is that they're infinitely malleable and can never be disproved. Once you have a mechanism that's designed to overcome any contradiction, you have a model that will last forever and, as we all know, the only models that last forever are ones that are true. Notice, though, the slight difference between this and the 'constructs' you used at school when proving geometric theorems. Then, you will remember, you used the construct at the beginning and went back at the end and rubbed it out *because it was a construct*. In less disciplined disciplines, you use constructs at the end to complete the proof and you make sure they can never be rubbed out. But one doesn't like to judge.

This particular dodge has always been with us. The earliest one on record is 'It's God's Will', which gives Him a fair amount of licence to smooth out theological anomalies, but a more strictly academic one with the greatest claim to seniority is Ptolemy's Epicycles. Ptolemy, when modelling the Solar System, suffered from two misconceptions – that the Earth was at the centre and that planetary orbits were circular – but even so, he managed to produce an entirely accurate predictor of the movements of the planets by the simple expedient of sticking as many circles on top of the orbital circles as were required to mimic the pattern, known from simple repetitive observation, of planetary movements. Job done.

The problem here is not that the model is bad, but that it's too good; a probe could be sent to Mars using Ptolemy's system. You can't judge a model solely by its efficacy. For that you need Occam's Razor: the model with the fewest 'constructs' that delivers the goods wins. Our present version requires just seven ellipses as against Ptolemy's several hundred circles and therefore wins. But it isn't that simple. The Ancients believed that circles were divine, and would therefore have regarded our ellipses as cheating; and were we to admit to them that actually our 'ellipses' are nothing of the kind, but chaotic paths changing constantly at the whim of passing bodies, they'd have laughed us out of court. The Newtonian System is far more complex than the Ptolemaic one (though it wins by describing a far more complex reality). The temptation, when you know the desired outcome, is to design a model that produces the desired outcome and then defend the model by pointing out that it produces the desired outcome. This is, in effect, what has happened to modern Darwinian Evolution. Biologists know the desired outcome – the species that are all around us – and they have as many 'theoretical common ancestors' as they care to construct to link all the known fossils with all the known living species. Plus they have a crucial advantage over Ptolemy, because measuring animal morphology is nowhere near as exacting as measuring planetary motions. With precious little in the way of imposed rules of any kind, biologists can get by with remarkably few constructs. One theoretical ancestral cat fits all. In fact the only thing that might pose a problem is if the real ancestral cat ever turned up.

Which brings us nicely to the *clever* clever clever clever bit: the theoretical ancestral cat can never be found! How do we know this? Well, let's see:

1. We have several dozen living cat species, all of whom could be the common ancestral cat but have been ruled out.

2. We have several fossil cat species that could be the common ancestral cat but have been ruled out, which leaves

3. all cat species that will be discovered from now until the end of time, either in the form of fossilised bones or actually prowling the rain forests of Borneo.

4. In order to qualify as the 'common ancestral cat', any member of category 3 would have to be either

5. **more** 'cattish' than all the failed cat-candidates so far, and since we have already been able to rule out candidates that can interbreed to produce sterile offspring, which is as close as two species can get and still be two species, that looks to be impossible; or

6. **less** 'cattish' than all the failed candidates so far, and since we have been able to rule out extinct candidates about which we know nothing apart from the fact that they were 'cattish', which is the lowest possible criterion that allows them still to be in the cat family in the first place, that too looks to be impossible.

However, there is one particular circumstance that does lead to this 'missing link' being found. Were the general public, bless 'em, to take an interest and start to protest at this ludicrous situation, you may be sure that one or other of the cat species would suddenly be ruled in. 'Extra! Extra! Ancestral Cat Found in Natural History Museum Basement. Read all about it. Free o'clock un' all the 'alftimes.'

This general argument applies to all species, and it's why the demand made of all Darwinians since 1859 – 'Show us a common ancestor' – is still answered 150 years later with: 'We will as soon as we find one.' This doesn't (exactly) render Darwinism null-and-void, but it does mean that, since the only thing that can disturb Darwinian Evolution is the discovery of a species that breaks the rules of Darwinian Evolution, we can all sleep soundly in our beds safe in the knowledge that our own chosen Super Creation Myth will be around for some little while yet. Of course, Darwinism will disappear as soon as its Hegelian function of overthrowing the previous paradigm, Biblical Creation Theory, has been satisfactorily completed; but being as how Creationist Middle America is the heartland of the world's current political and intellectual superpower, we can all take comfort that this titanic battle between warring midgets should hold the line for our lifetimes. Nor should we ignore the possibility that Darwinian Evolution might turn out to be true, in which case it will last even longer.

All kinds of loopiness break out whenever ancestral forms outlive their ancestral duties, and they're a constant bugbear for any time-based academic subject unable to agree an efficient method of cauterisation. My own earliest exposure to this syndrome was:

'Mum, does Guernsey belong to England?'
'No, England belongs to Guernsey.'

'How do you work that one out?'

'Guernsey was part of Normandy at the time of the Conquest and as far as we're concerned Queen Elizabeth is still the Duke of Normandy.'

The basic difficulty is always the same: how to place a definite ceiling on what went before when 'further research is needed' is being employed to cover all the other loose ends that arise when imposing *a priori* schemes on the real world. In other words, it has been a structural flaw for the whole of the post-Enlightenment academic era. For instance, when geologists of the late 18th century realised that the rock strata provided a rough chronology of the Earth – a layer of chalk on top of a layer of sandstone meant that the sandstone must have been laid down before the chalk – this was quite sufficient to over-throw Divine Creation Theory, in which, as it were, nothing comes before everything in the Earth's history. So immediately the rock strata became epochal in both senses. Now, being committed to a rock strata paradigm from Day One has had very profound implications for Academic Geology. For a start, it more or less obliged the early geologists to go in for a bit of Creationism on their own account in order to come up with the magisterial but entirely bogus timeline of Jurassic, Middle Cretaceous, Upper Late Pliocene and all the rest of the eye-popping labels that so lovingly sum up this our Earth. Actually it must have been a bit of *Divine* Creationism, because when centuries later geologists found a way of dating the rocks quite independently using atomic decay, blow me, it turned out the Old Pioneers scratching around in Old Devonian mudshales had got everything completely spot on!

159

Is that foresight, or is that hindsight? Neither, say Applied Epistemologists, it's horseshite.

Not only did the early geologists have no way of dating rock strata on an absolute scale, they had no way of tying in rock strata in one part of the world with rock strata in another. All they could do, in the time-honoured way, was 'to proffer a provisional scheme that best reflected the known facts' and wait for academic ossification to set in. Since 'the known facts' as far as the Early Pioneers were concerned amounted to some similarities in rock-types at comparable depths in north-western Europe, it's not surprising that their Universal History of the Earth was somewhat skewed to the parochial. This may be a weakness in terms of the strict Pursuit of Truth, but it's a strength when it comes to developing nascent academic disciplines because it meant that generations of British and French students could be sent off 'into the field' to prove to themselves that, yes, the Cambrian did indeed underlie the Devonian because the bloke at the front with the biggest hammer pointed out what was the Cambrian and what was the Devonian. Actually, British students might well have been looking at a different Devonian and a different Cambrian from the French students since they had no way of dovetailing across time and across the Channel, but this didn't matter so long as both British and French students dutifully memorised the sequence Cambrian/Devonian. You might ask why the French students did not, as the French are wont to do, insist on their rocks being called Armorican and Dordognian, but that would have been rather to blow the gaff, because so long as every geological student in every country in the world marched round with an identical 'map o' the rocks', he could name every stratum in his own country. Remember, without absolute dating, this is an entirely arbitrary matter: Jurassic might be at the surface in Argentina (because of erosion) but several thousand feet down in China (because of deposition), so it was strictly up to the natives what constituted Jurassic. Paradigm Centre didn't mind, so long as what they called Jurassic was above what they called Permian and below what they called Cretaceous.

There *was* one check that was supposed to keep the system honest: each layer had to have certain characteristics depending on the state of the Earth when the rocks were laid down. Trouble was, the local characteristics of Argentina tended to differ more from China than the Permian differed from the Jurassic. Bugger, what to do? Answer: find a marker that could be used world-wide. And they had the ideal candidate – coal – which, naturally enough, was laid down in the hot and humid 'Carboniferous' era. What, hot and humid the world over and never before or since? Well, let's not forget, it was a very nascent science. Anyway, it worked well enough. As we have seen, the important thing about getting an academic subject launched is to have an agreed scheme, since then it's merely a question of ensuring that all geology students are taught the new scheme by rote (and no non-geologist has a hope of distinguishing his Pliocene from his Pleistocene), then ensuring that anybody teaching geology must be an ex-geology student, then ensuring that all other academic disciplines are forbidden from dating the rock strata independently, and finally ensuring that anything within the rock strata of interest to other disciplines (minerals, fossils, hominid remains, human artefacts) is handled by special 'bridging' subjects (mineralogy, palaeontology, palaeo-anthropology and archaeology) that are committed in advance to geological paradigms.

All would have been well but for one inconvenient fact. There happened to be a group of people outside the control of geology who actually knew rather more than any geologist about coal-bearing rock strata, and that was the coal-miners. At first there was no conflict. The geologists had, after all, originally used coal-mining data from north-west Europe to establish the Carboniferous layer in the first place. But as mining techniques improved, as exploration areas moved away from Europe, well dangee me, the bastards kept on finding coal outside the Carboniferous layer. No problem! Increase the width of the Carboniferous Era to include the new coal deposits! That was OK for a while, but pretty soon the Carboniferous was twice the size of all the other eras and still coal kept turning up in other levels. Time to call a halt and quietly ditch the notion of a warm, damp, swampy world covered with giant plants busy laying down coal deposits. (I say 'quietly ditch' because everybody still believes it in a vague sort of way.) Thankfully, the geological industry largely gave up on coal and moved into oil. 'Ooh yes', they said, 'Pay us a lot of petrodollars and we'll tell you exactly where to bore your drill holes.' And they were right! Regular as clockwork, once every ten holes, they found oil (which paid for the other nine and plenty over for everybody). In fact they've been getting it right – that is, getting it right once every ten goes – ever since they started in the 1860s, and that's still the figure today. So either oil occurs randomly in 10 per cent of the Earth's crust or we're in the middle of an astounding run of coincidences. Let's hope it's the latter, because otherwise it would mean my dog has the same chance of sniffing out oil deposits as Exxon, and I can't afford to pay him that kind of money.

None of this is to deny that the work of the early geologists was enormously beneficial. The Earth Sciences would scarcely exist today were it not for a bunch of people agreeing a nominal skeleton scheme upon which they and their successors could build a really useful structure. The villains of the story are *today's* geologists, the ones who continue to insist that the nominal skeleton scheme first sketched in by the pioneers actually exists in the real world, thereby condemning their subject to a dwarfish existence constantly hog-tied to a faulty paradigm. That's the real tragedy of these false paradigms. One doesn't terribly mind a bunch of bozos believing fairy stories at our expense (the Church of England is a great public comfort), but one does mind the Earth Sciences being a pathetic intellectual rump living on the glory – as well as the theories – of their noble forebears.

As good children of the Enlightenment, none of us can truly conceive of an aeon-free world, any more than our great-great-grandfathers could conceive of a God-free one, but even so, there are ways of finessing time when deconstructing time-based academic paradigms. Evolutionary biologists, for instance, could take a self-denying ordinance and deal only with presently existing species and then, by using DNA number-crunching, work out a set of properly scientific evolutionary relationships. This would gradually replace the subjective family trees that they have hitherto compiled by the use of the broad brush of animal morphology and peer-review – and it's deeply suspicious how few changes the 20th-century Genetic Revolution has had on the 18th-century Linnaean System. It seems that dear old fumbling Linnaeus (and I suppose one would have to include dear old cheating Mendel) are more divinely-touched savants who magically seemed to get everything right first time, every time. The geologists, of course, should never again use a humanly-named epoch and should turn instead to a strictly date-based system. They will be amazed how much the past changes when instead of the Ordovician giving way to the Silurian, 500 million years BP becomes 499 million years BP. It prevents rote learning for a start. A classroom of questioning students ... could be fun.

But what, pray, has all this to do with British history? Consider what happens if the evolutionary nexus between English and Anglo-Saxon is broken. Where does that leave English, language and people? Firmly mired in the bottomless pit, of course. If English did *not* arrive in Britain with Horsa and Hengist in the 5th century AD, then it has no chronology; it means (for certain) that Julius Caesar was greeted in English by the locals, it means (for maybe) that Stonehenge was built by English-speakers, it might mean (it can't be ruled out) that human language was invented in Britain. These are strangely discomforting thoughts. But to avoid the bottomless pit, English has to be plugged into something; and if that something is not to be Anglo-Saxon and via Anglo-Saxon to German (High, Low or Middling) and via German into the cosy assumptions – i.e. the trackless wastes – of Eastern Europe and Hither Asia ... then what? Then where? Then when? At best, it means more 'reconstructed' ancestral languages, more dotted lines, more proto- question marks, but this time so far off the beaten track of solid data that the demand 'More research needed!' may not necessarily lead to its usual corollary 'More researchers needed!'

The academic search for English roots bodes ill thus far. Generally speaking, any tripartite division in academia is a pre-sentiment that the Three Card Trick is being played, and we have a prime example with Old, Middle and Modern English. This particular triptych is a typical artefact of scholarship:

1. It's self-evidently true that anything in a condition of change over a long period of time (such as a spoken language) will have a history of being old, not-quite-so-old and bang-up-to-date.

2. It's no less self-evidently true that any sub-division you care to choose will be demonstrably true in the limited sense that each sub-division will be measurably different from the one before and the one after.

3. Selecting an arbitrary scheme that has precisely a beginning, a middle and an end appeals to anybody who likes a good story, i.e. all human beings.

Academics ought to be formally forbidden from adopting arbitrary tripartite systems on these grounds alone – and not just academics: the constant urge to divide societies into upper, middle and lower classes appears to be part of the same human condition. Despite the fact that there are entire academic departments devoted to Old, Middle and Modern English, it's a straightforward matter to demonstrate that none of these actually exists in nature. (The languages, that is; the departments expand exponentially.)

You might be puzzled to be told that Modern English

doesn't exist, given that you speak it, but stop being puzzled and start thinking. What actually is Modern English? Or, to put it another way, what *isn't* Modern English? French isn't, for a start. I can't have a worthwhile conversation with a French-speaker, even after studying their blessèd language for five years. (Nor can any other English-speaker in my position, nor can any French-speaker who spent five years studying English. Can somebody tell me what the purpose of this great bi-national effort was? Oh … it trained our minds … oh, right … thanks.) In fact, I can't comprehend any other language on Earth, not even a New Guinean pidgin packed with borrowings from English. On the other hand, I *can* have a meaningful conversation with every single English-speaker on Earth, be they a Jamaican Yardie, Arkansas trailer-trash or the Queen of England. (The Jamaican might be able to switch into an incomprehensible patois, but that's another language; he's perfectly able to speak English too.) How far does this 'meaningful conversation' test apply historically? Well, let's see … I can follow the increasingly strangulated vowels of BBC English all the way back to the birth of radio; in fact I can understand all English I have ever heard, going back to Edison phonographs. After that I have to rely on written English to judge my comprehension levels. Gladstone's speeches? The Declaration of Independence? Mrs Malaprop? Restoration Revenge Drama? No difficulties whatsoever. Only when we get as far back as Shakespeare do I encounter the first problem: I doubt that I could read the First Folio – the typeface is way too gothick. However, I can mostly understand the plays, even if I would prefer, in my philistine way, that He would speak plainer. As we amble back even further in time through *Gawain and the Green Knight*, the *Canterbury Tales* and *Piers Plowman*, the spelling gets completely out of hand; but once that's put right, I find that – apart from perhaps one word in 50 requiring the glossary – I am entirely up to speed with proceedings. And that's as far back as 'Modern' English goes. We don't know what was being spoken by ordinary 'English'-speakers before then, because our sources are too sketchy and too ambiguous.

Either going vertically through history or horizontally across the world, there doesn't seem to be anything that can properly be called 'Modern' English; there's just English, plain and simple, a language that I can speak and write and share with every other English-speaker. Yes, it's true that there's Shakespearean English and American English and Jamaican English and even the Queen's English; there are, when you come to think of it, as many sub-divisions of English as there are English-speakers, but all of us can make ourselves understood to one another, whereas (unless we have specifically made the effort) none of us can understand any other language. There's nothing weird about this. One's language, after all, is expressly designed so that you can communicate with total strangers. Every day you meet somebody new and have need to communicate with them. And unless that person speaks English, you won't be able to. So that person makes damned sure he can speak English, because he's just met you and will need to communicate with you. That's why, contrary to the vapourings of the linguists, languages are incredibly steady-state institutions. Yes, they are changing on a daily basis; yes, they are developing at colossal speed in times of great technical change; yes, they change to reflect cultural

167

diversity; no, they don't change at the institutional level of communication. If I don't know a particular neologism, if I'm not au fait with some arcane new usage, I'll ask. Just like if I'm chatting to Geoff Chaucer I'll reach for the glossary. Whether I could communicate with English-speaking Stonehenge-builders is, I admit, a bit more problematical; but whether I could or whether I couldn't, I doubt we'd be able to agree just when 'Modern' English began. I expect they'd say it was some time in the Iron Age.

So it rather looks as if Modern English, the third card, 'the effect' at the end of this particular cause-and-effect story, doesn't exist except and unless it can be both connected to and then differentiated from at least one other kind of 'English'. Let us then turn to the first card, the 'cause' that set this story running, 'Old English'. This most certainly does not exist – it's just Anglo-Saxon, plain and simple, and even academics acknowledge this. But notice the brazenness of the sleight-of-hand here: there's no doubt that a language called Anglo-Saxon exists; there's equally no doubt that a language called Old English exists in the sense that English is quite old; so academics have, with a simple stroke of the pen, declared Anglo-Saxon to be Old English. Nobody has ever been able to establish a causal connection between Anglo-Saxon and 'Modern' English. All that can be demonstrated is a *linguistic* relationship between Anglo-Saxon and 'Modern' English, in exactly the same way as Dutch, Swedish and Danish are linguistically related to English – and nobody has ever claimed that Dutch, Swedish or Danish is Old English.

There is, however, one vital attribute that Anglo-Saxon has that Dutch, Swedish and Danish do not have: Anglo-Saxon is an *extinct* language. Sounds familiar? Yes, that's right, it's dead-cat-bounce time again. Despite the similarities between all the world's languages, despite their apparent longevity, despite the fact that we know one language often gives rise to another, the languages we hear around us are supposed, by some weird concatenation of circumstance, to be evolved overwhelmingly from dead languages as opposed to one another. Wherever a fossil language is available (Anglo-Saxon, Latin, Ancient Greek, Sanskrit, etc.), that is named as the ancestor; if none is available, one is made up (Indic, proto-Slavic, Altaic, etc.). This is exactly the same as the absurd position that biologists have found themselves in:

1. We know that evolution takes place since, unless each is a separate creation, there are millions of species and thousands of languages all around us.

2. We know that all species/languages have the capacity to give rise to other species/languages.

3. By an amazing set of coincidences, none of the species/languages that exist today have given rise to other species/languages.

There's a good reason, though, for this assumption by our linguistic masters. Consider the embarrassment if some remnant Anglo-Saxon population was discovered still living in some Shangri-La valley in the Erz Gebirge. They would still be speaking recognisable Anglo-Saxon because *every discrete language population of which we have a continuous record speaks the same recognisable language they always did*, which would raise the uncomfortable, unanswerable, question of why their compatriots in

England are the sole population group we know of that is not. But remember the operative term here is 'continuous'. As we have seen over and over again, once we have a *discontinuous* record, when for some reason or another the written record is not available, then any old creation myth tripe can be foisted.

But anyway, foist it has been, so now all that's required for officialdom to tie Old English to Modern English is the careful insertion of the Queen of Diamonds and the Three Card Trick will be complete. Enter 'Middle English'. Notice that officially Middle English is both an extinct language (nobody nowadays speaks it) and a reconstructed one (scholars have had to piece it together from wisps of surviving literature), but as to whether it actually ever existed in history, whether it was actually spoken by a group of living, breathing individuals who once walked the Earth, you should, when deciding the truth of the matter, bear in mind that the only evidence we have derives from the written material of:

1. English-speakers of the 12th and 13th centuries who may have wished to write things down in their own language but had no way of doing so except by using either a Latin or an Anglo-Saxon script to convey the appropriate sounds.

2. Anglo-Saxon-speakers of the 12th and 13th centuries who may have wished to write things down in their own language, except that this was no longer taught in any schools or monasteries, which had, thanks to the Normans, all gone over to Latin and French.

3. Academics of the 19th and 20th centuries who were

supremely anxious to find 'the missing link' between English and Anglo-Saxon and were therefore on the lookout for any written texts from the 12th and 13th centuries that betray the slightest trace, however tenuous and however ambiguous, of any degree of overlap between Anglo-Saxon and Modern English.

And, as usual, just to clinch matters, nothing further now can ever be discovered that will disturb this situation, because it's exceedingly unlikely that any texts of any sort from the 12th and 13th centuries will turn up at this late date. So the academic die is cast; but anybody who isn't a Middle English specialist but is eager to find out how easily quite intelligent people can manage to convince themselves that something they want to exist can seem to self-evidently exist even though it doesn't exist should Google 'Middle English' and browse the results. But beware, once you fall into a community of True Believers you have to keep reminding yourself that the casually authoritative tone of everyone around you is not in itself evidence. Just keep asking yourself every time a text is presented to you: 'Is this really a half-way house between Anglo-Saxon and Modern English?' You only have to answer this question once in the affirmative and they are right and I am wrong.

But surprisingly, the conjuring into existence of Middle English is not primarily to tie 'Modern' English to Anglo-Saxon – that could be achieved by the time-honoured ruse adopted by all evolutionary systems of joining them up with a dotted line and then with a nod and a wink assuring everyone that the link really is established but modesty demands a scrupulous indication of uncertainty. Middle English is actually necessary to solve a much more pressing problem: explaining the Latinate content of English. This is an absolute requirement, because the situation as orthodoxy understands it is that:

1. c. 400 AD there is a population living in Britain speaking Old Welsh, a language with a negligible Latinate content;

2. c. 500 AD along comes another population speaking Anglo-Saxon, a language with a negligible Latinate content;

3. and between them they produce a population speaking English, a language with an enormous Latinate content.

Usually, when explaining any aberrant content of a given language, linguists find it quite sufficient to draw together whatever useful bits and pieces historians can provide them with. In the case of Latinisation, a long list of vehicles might be paraded – the Roman Empire, the Catholic Church, the introduction of civilisation, writing, cultural dissemination, trade, trickle-down, etc., etc. – and then with a wave of the peer-review wand, the problem is declared solved. In short, the 'It Just Happened' school of history. But to be on the safe side, as we have seen, orthodoxy always makes sure that 'it just happens' during a Dark Age when there's a convenient hiatus in the written record. This is completely foolproof, because historians can rely on linguists to assure everyone that it did happen and linguists can rely on historians to assure everyone how it happened, and since they're all singing from the same paradigm hymn-sheet, there's no way in for objecting outsiders.

With one exception. If you remember your table from page 12, the Anglo-Saxons were unique among all the Dark Age tribes in getting their language adopted by the locals, and since the Anglo-Saxons were literate from very early on, England becomes the only country in Europe with a continuous written record in the same language from very soon after the Romans right up until the present day (according to tenured authority),
which means
the changeover occurred in fully historical times,
which means
we know when the changeover was supposed to have taken place,
which means
we know what the language situation was before and after the changeover took place.

So in the unique case of English, the historians know more or less precisely what was going on, and the poor old linguists can't just bundle together the usual list of *maybes*, *could-bes* and *what-the-hell-let's-stick-it-in-anyways*, but instead are actually constrained by real, genuine, on-the-ground, in-the-literature facts. We know what Anglo-Saxon was like and when, we know what English was like and when, and we know that the only half-decent vehicle-for-Latinisation that took place between Anglo-Saxon and English was the Norman Conquest. This is unbelievably infuriating from a Latinisation point of view, because the Normans

1. did not introduce civilisation into England – theirs was a 'civilisation' all but indistinguishable from the Anglo-Saxons' own;

2. did not introduce writing – Anglo-Saxon became a written language several hundred years before the Norman Conquest;

3. did not introduce Latin – the Anglo-Saxons had been using Latin, and presumably ransacking it for whatever loan-words they felt to be necessary, long before the Normans left Norway, never mind Normandy;

4. did not introduce Roman Christianity – it was Romanised Anglo-Saxon missionaries that mostly converted the originally Scandinavian Normans;

5. did not introduce vernacular writing – the Normans' switch from using Latin to written French for temporal purposes in England was almost exactly contemporaneous with the emergence of written vernacular English in England.

However, historians can't altogether be blamed for this apparently impossible situation. Looked at from their point of view, they can only argue:

1. We know that English is an evolved form of Anglo-Saxon (the linguists have assured us this is the case).

2. We know what Anglo-Saxon was like up to the 12th century (we have historical documents to that effect).

3. We know what English was like in the 14th century (we have historical documents to that effect).

4. The only radical difference between 12th-century England and 14th-century England was the new Norman administration.

5. We know that the Normans spoke a Latinate language.

6. So that's it then. It must be. There's no getting round it. We're naturally sorry if this presents problems, contradictions, paradoxes, evidential black holes or whatever, but since that's what happened, that's what happened, and there's nothing we can do about it. Blame history, not historians.

Such is the faith we repose in the conjurors – and such is the faith the conjurors repose in themselves – that when they say with complete assurance, 'Trust us, the Norman Conquest is the Queen of Diamonds', we do exactly that. Remember, this is a national creation myth; we *want* to lose our money. Otherwise it's the Pit for us.

To vary the metaphor, Middle English acts as junction box: Anglo-Saxon goes in at one end, Modern English comes out the other. Of course it's a very special kind of junction box with hardly any moving parts (there are very few 'Middle English' documents), and one whose innards may be inspected only by registered experts (Middle English specialists), but there it stands, forever preventing advance, unless Applied Epistemology can come up with a superior junction box – a better explanation as to why English has a one-third Latinate content – and since we're the only people who are actually looking, I suppose we had better do just that. Let's begin with this intriguing case of academic double-standards:

1. One-third of English words are cognate with French words, a fact that has led academic linguists to conclude, self-evidently, that English has been heavily influenced by French in its formative years.

2. Two-thirds of French words are cognate with English words, a fact that has never led academic linguists to conclude anything at all.

Now, as any academic linguist would concede, there is only one circumstance in which Language A's vocabulary can be so heavily cognate with Language B, and that's when there is a causal connection between A and B, either directly or indirectly. So, if French did not 'cause' the Latinate content of English, we must, at last, grasp the radical nettle and conclude that English 'caused' French, i.e. that French is an evolved form of English.

I should, at this point, state for the record that I do not myself *believe* that French is an evolved form of English. This is for two reasons:

1. There is no clear, unequivocal evidence that it is.

2. I do not wish to be *Rainbow Warrior*ed by the Deuxième Bureau acting as the executive arm of the Académie Française.

However, what I do believe is that there is a *prima facie* case that French is an evolved form of English. The argument relies entirely on an application of Occam's Razor: my model is simpler than their model when it comes to explaining the agreed facts, and therefore, whilst both models may be wrong, it is irrational in our present state of knowledge to prefer the orthodox model to the Applied Epistemological one.

Orthodoxy holds that the language situation in Western Europe came into existence like this:

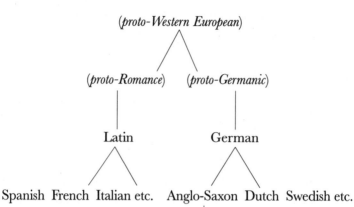

Quite elegant, but to achieve this elegance certain liberties
have had to be taken:

1. Because the two 'creation myth' languages, Latin and
   German, are linguistically so far apart, two complete
   layers of 'reconstructed languages' (proto-Western
   European; proto-Romance, proto-Germanic) have had
   to be inserted to tie them together.

2. These reconstructed languages are made from combining their daughter languages, thus inserting the conclusion into the problem.

3. Though there's plenty of time – thousands of years –
   for the general scheme to unfold, time has had to be
   summarily telescoped quite unrealistically into a couple
   of hundred years on both branches, to 'evolve' Latin
   into the Romance languages and to 'evolve' Anglo-
   Saxon into English.

177

4. There's no explanation for why the Romance languages are more like one another than their common ancestor, Latin. A further reconstructed language, 'Ancestral Modern Romance'/Vulgar Latin, would have to be inserted between Latin and Spanish, French, Italian, etc. to make the model conform to our normal understanding of language development.

5. There's no explanation as to why English has such a high Latinate content when it's on the Germanic branch.

6. There's no explanation as to why English is so much larger than all the other languages.

In other words, according to Occam, it's probably complete rubbish. Let's see whether our own hypothesis works any better:

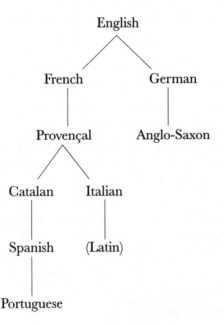

Just as elegant, but let's check the liberties:

1. No 'reconstructed' languages are required. What you hear is what you get.

2. There are no time constraints or telescoping since we have no record of when any of these changes occurred, except that we have many thousands of years for the whole process to unfold.

3. It explains why all the modern Romance languages are more alike one to another than any of them are to Latin.

4. It explains why English has such a high Latinate content, or rather it explains why Latin has such a high English content.

5. It offers a possible explanation as to why English is larger than the other languages (it's older).

Not bad, but what of the difficulties? The most obvious one (apart from getting your mind round such a shocking novelty) is that of the relationship between German and French. While the most important rule of language evolution – that daughter languages are overwhelmingly cognate with mother languages – is obeyed in the case both of English and French and of English and German, the second most important rule – that sister languages are reasonably cognate with one another – is hard to reconcile in the case of French and German. As we have seen, one is almost entirely 'Latinate', the other not at all.

But, as we have also seen, 'Latinate' may not be quite what we have always supposed it to be; and it is agreed, even by orthodoxy, that all German and French words are reasonably cognate in the looser sense of sharing Western Indo-European roots. But that is not satisfactory for our purposes, so we must consider carefully what 'reasonably cognate' actually means in the evolution of languages. The first thing to bear in mind is that, although language family trees are set out as if they were human family trees, they are not. With human beings, two siblings bear the same general relationship to each other as each does to either parent (50 per cent shared genes, 50 per cent non-shared genes), so it's proper to arrange matters thus:

Father   Mother

Sister ——————— Brother

This isn't the case with languages, because languages split off chaotically, in different directions, giving rise to a relationship more like:

French ← ← ← English → → → **German**

… where French and German, though sibling languages, are much further away from one another than either is from its English parent. In practice, the distance will be greater still, because the splits will (presumably) have happened at different times, giving us:

French ← ← ← Very Ancient English

Not-Quite-So-Ancient English → → → **German**

How much English altered in the hundreds or thousands of years between the putative budding-off of French and then German (or German and then French) is so difficult to evaluate that it tells us one of the reasons why time-based academic subjects try very hard to opt for extinct forebears rather than living ones: extinct languages are 'fixed'. They provide certainty. The Latin of Cicero is much the same as the Latin of Gregory of Tours which is much the same as the Latin that 19th-century philologists can mine for evidence of the Latin origins of French. Without that degree of certainty, could there even be an academic subject? Probably, but having to cope with living, breathing, changing languages does make studying them fearfully messy. And oftentimes downright paradoxical: take, for example, the relationship between Norwegian and Icelandic. We know from historical evidence that Iceland was colonised by Norwegians, giving us the apparent relationship:

Norwegian

|

Icelandic

We also know from the Sagas that modern Icelandic is virtually identical to Old Norse, and Old Norse is held to be the forebear of Modern Norwegian. So it's also entirely correct to construct a family language-tree, on strictly linguistic grounds, that reads:

Icelandic

|

Norwegian

An odd inversion, but orthodoxy would sniff and say: 'Languages on remote islands don't change very much, so while Norwegian moved on, Icelandic did not.' Which is fair enough, except that their whole theory relies on ultra-rapid language change in the Dark Ages when, as it were, everyone is on a remote island – but doubtless they have a theory for that as well. What we can say with fair confidence is that if there were no historical evidence and hence modern linguists were simply confronted with Icelandic and Norwegian, they would reconstruct 'proto-Nordic' out of the common elements of both languages; they would certainly not come up with Modern Icelandic. As it happens, the Icelandic/Norwegian nexus holds the key to the true history of Europe, but that is for another time.

For our purposes here, we might break the tyranny of time by visualising *place*. Just as knowing that Icelanders have physically removed themselves across the ocean from Norwegians assists us in assessing their true relationship, so conceptualising English-, French- and German-speakers on the move can do likewise. We might, for instance, posit some great cavalcade of ox-carts travelling west out of the Urals, bearing a tribe of people speaking, for want of a better term, *proto-Western European*. Once across the Elbe, a bunch of them leave the wagon-train, colonise the land, and over the next *n* thousand years evolve this proto-Western European into German, and then send out off-shoots and off-shoots of off-shoots that end up speaking Dutch, Swedish, and so on. The rest of the wagon-train crosses the Rhine, whereupon another bunch get off and start evolving proto-Western European into French, whose off-shoots and off-shoots of off-shoots go on to develop

Italian, Spanish, Portuguese and so forth. The remainder stay on until they reach the end of the road in the British Isles (not that they were necessarily isles at this time), whereupon they sit tight as proto-Western European gradually becomes what we nowadays call English.

This, though, points up another difficulty with evolutionary schemes: we might just as easily say that proto-Western European 'evolves' into English, rather than 'becomes' English; but 'evolves' is normally reserved for situations where another language is budded off, as for instance Spanish 'evolves' from French, though really it would be truer to say only that French and Spanish 'changed differentially'. For all we know, present-day Spanish might be closer to proto-Western European than present-day French – or indeed English. Evolutionary schemes tend always to suffer from the fact that, in the real world, it is things at the end of the line that might change least – on the Icelandic model – and therefore be most representative, whereas the academics operating the system much prefer the mainstream languages to play this role. Indeed, this is essential if you are relying on a tree-trunk-with-branches model, as all evolutionary schemes do.

But this ox-cart model is only a restating of the orthodox assumption that everything travels westwards, that everything comes out of the heart of Asia, and more distantly 'out of Africa'. As selective contrarians, Applied Epistemologists would probably argue 'as above, so below', i.e. the same sequential evidence would fit a west-to-east model in which everyone arrives by boat along the Atlantic coast and spreads (no doubt on ox-carts) across Europe and into Asia. Just as, though this takes us beyond the scope of this book, we tend to the belief that the genetic evidence demonstrates clearly that the African populations were the *last* to arrive rather than the first. Only Applied Epistemology points out that actually everyone's mitochrondrial DNA is exactly as old as everyone else's and that therefore variations within it are much more likely to arise from the most movement across the Earth's surface rather than the least. But then only Applied Epistemology has the temerity to point out just why this perfectly common-sense assumption has been stood on its head by geneticists: if you were trying to get a new academic subject accepted, would you choose a model (Out-of-Africa) that would evoke admiring cries of 'Thank God, at last some scientific underpinning for something which fits all our paradigms (and is a useful piece of liberal anti-racism to boot). Here, have a Chair in Genetic Anthropology'; or would you propose a model (Into-Africa) that would receive derisive dismissal: 'Sorry, you've got that all wrong. It contradicts all the evidence. Come back when you've got some results that make sense in the real world.' And while we're on the subject of political correctness, I suppose I ought to point out that an Atlantic origin for the Indo-Europeans is what the Thule Society advocated. Do you honestly want to line up behind Adolf Hitler? Yes, say Applied Epistemologists, if that's what it takes. And we'd like the trains to run on time too.

Everybody goes round muttering 'All history is subjective', but nobody goes round muttering 'Hey, that means the history I personally believe is subjective'. It's fair to say that the history profession tries to address this problem by demanding that every statement be supported by a piece of contemporary documentation. It's also fair to acknowledge that this has largely done the trick where documentation is profuse – national histories are pretty good nowadays in Western Europe and America. *Sectional* history is of course quite a different matter – the history of blacks, women, trade unions, ordinary people, ordinary things are ludicrously partisan, but that's only to be expected while the pioneers are still at work. It's where the written record gives out that the real problems lie. Historians seem to give up. They just assume that the creation myths are true, or at any rate that they are somebody else's business. What can they do? Give up being historians, that's what. Cease relying on the written record, annex whatever parts of genetics, palaeo-anthropology or linguistics are relevant, and take proper control of the past.

Anybody who finds the material in *The History of Britain Revealed* interesting enough to wish to follow things up should head for

www.applied-epistemology.org

where they will find a whole bunch of people following up this and various other strands of organised human thought that require radical revision. However, you are strongly advised not to Google 'Applied Epistemology', because there you will be greeted by thousands of entries from and about people who claim to be involved in Applied Epistemology but who in fact have hijacked this very useful term to open yet another interminable branch in that utterly useless area of academic endeavour, Philosophy. Real Applied Epistemology deals with real trees in real forests that exist, so far as we know, whether we are observing them or not. Yes, yes, you believe that 'so far as we know' is a frightfully important qualification. On second thoughts, don't bother to join us.

Index

replace Romano-British 10–11,
17, 32–3, 37, 55, 77, 96, 97
replacement by Normans 6, 10,
60, 98, 173
in Scotland 23, 34, 37
unique in annals 12, 56
Anglo-Saxonists 3, 45, 50, 56–7,
80–1, 170–1
animal words 134
anomalies
in Applied Epistemology 7–8
in cause and effect 140–4
Celtic Fringe (Anomaly Two)
14–39, 96–8
changing everyone's language
(Anomaly One) 10–14, 96
forming a matrix 61
'gap years' (Anomaly Three)
125–9
geographical pattern of speakers
116
'Hide-the-Anomaly' playbook 118
human settlement (Anomaly
Four) 52–7, 98–101
in the humanities 93–4
Latin as written language
(Anomaly Four) 129–32
'Latin quarter' (Anomaly Two)
120–5
Latinate content of English 133
et seq.
loan-words in English (Anomaly
Five) 58–60, 101
(non-)morphology of languages
(Anomaly Three) 39–52, 98
in orthodox history 6–9, 76–85
'plus ça change' (Anomaly One)
114–20
in pre-history 67–71
in Romance languages 112–14

theological 155
in vertical and horizontal subjects
76
anthropology 3, 69, 99, 184
palaeo- 68, 162, 185
Antonine Wall 20, 22
Applied Epistemology
Anglo-Saxon Chronicle 48
basic methodology 4
Blue Riband committees 80
British history 38
'careful ignoral' 76
cause and effect 140–1
Celtic fringe 18
Chaucer 45
cognitive dissonance 149
English-speakers easily conquered
32
European language lacuna 13
falling masonry 154
French derived from English 176
Gaul's language 110
genetics of British population 88
geological paradigms 160
German Anglo-Saxons 56–7
historians cutting corners 68
history of French language 145
Hitler, Adolf 184
Irish languages 26
junction between pre-history and
science 67
Latin conversion of Romance
area 121–2
linguistic methodology 43
linguistic patterns 31
Mercury's orbit 8
Middle English 175
mitochondrial DNA 184
origin of the Indo-Europeans
183